"A terrifying tapestry of demonic folklore, history, and first-person reportage, *Hunting Demons* is Sylvia Shults's masterpiece. Woven with the eye of an anthropologist, the openness of a true believer, and the heart of a storyteller, *Hunting Demons* should be an indispensable addition to the bookshelves of all aficionados of the paranormal."
Jay Bonansinga, author of *Lucid* and *The Walking Dead: Invasion*

"This book is an eye opener to good and evil, right and wrong, living and dead and the others, the minions of evil's dominion. Great read on oppression and the obstacle filled road to where freedom lies. Every spiritual, paranormal or non sensitive individual will get something out of this documented work of truth that will change you for a lifetime. Great job Sylvia in finding the literary truth of the root of the matter and outline of steps to take for a paranormal investigations freedom. We'll be referencing your book to our new and past clients. Excellent read and brutally honest in the subject of demonic oppression and the spirit world around us."
Daniel Beck Mewhinney, founder of SOCALPRS, the dangers of the paranormal project at theDOTPproject.com, radio host at www.paranormaldestinations.com, public speaker, TV talent and sensitive investigator and spiritual advocate for life. We are never alone...

"Sylvia Shults is the best nonfiction paranormal writer I've ever read. Her wealth of history and paranormal knowledge combines with a literate and very approachable writing style to seduce even the skeptical."
Tamara Thorne, author of *The Cliffhouse Haunting*

A TRUE STORY OF THE DARK SIDE OF THE SUPERNATURAL

HUNTING DEMONS

BY SYLVIA SHULTS

American Hauntings Ink & Whitechapel Press

Note: Due to the sensitive nature of this material, some names and identifying characteristics have been changed. The stories, however, are true.

© Copyright 2015 by Sylvia Shults

All Rights Reserved, including the right to copy or reproduce this book, or portions thereof, in any form, without express permission from the author and publisher.

Original Cover Artwork Designed by
© Copyright 2015 by April Slaughter

This Book is Published By:
Whitechapel Press
American Hauntings Ink
Jacksonville, Illinois   1-888-446-7859
Visit us on the Internet at http: www.whitechapelpress.com

First Edition - August 2015
ISBN: 1-892523-96-5

Printed in the United States of America

PROLOGUE

Linda wanted the screaming to stop.

Linda had been a ghost hunter for years. She had heard whispers, groans, the thump of disembodied footsteps. She had heard the ghostly giggle of a dead patient in the cemetery at the Peoria State Hospital. She had heard a plaintive whimper in the basement of an abandoned house – "No one has ever talked to me." She had heard the whispered thank you of a spirit released to go to the Light.

But she had never heard the crazed shrieking of three demonic entities all at once, three demons yelling over each other to be the one to heap the most abuse on this pathetic human. The voices were loud, grating, dripping with venomous hate. Linda clapped her hands over her ears, but the voices still rang around her head. She couldn't escape the shouts and curses that drilled into her mind, into her soul. A tear slipped down her cheek as she gritted her teeth against the abuse.

"Worship Satan! There is no God – we're your only god now! Give up, give in, give your soul to us! We're gonna take your soulllll!"

Linda fell to her knees. The carpet in her living room bit at the skin of her knees as she landed, but she barely noticed. She clasped her hands in the ancient gesture of pleading and begged, pleaded, wept to her God, "Lord, please, please make it stop! I didn't want this, I swear I didn't want this. Please, God, make it STOP!"

PART ONE
HUNTING DEMONS

1. A GHOST SEEKER'S EDUCATION

There are ghosts everywhere.

This is something I have come to believe, just as firmly as I believe that when I flick a switch, a room will flood with light. My acceptance of the presence of the spirit world took a lot longer than the knowledge of the easy availability of electricity.

I learned to read at a very young age. By the time I got to grade school, my tastes were fairly wide-ranging, but I had discovered a particular addiction to the weird. I devoured every book I could find on anything mysterious – the Loch Ness Monster, unexplained disappearances, spontaneous combustion, time travel, time slips, the moving coffins of Barbados – the grosser and spookier the better. Tales of Egyptian tomb curses would keep me enthralled for hours. And ever since I heard about the Oak Island Money Pit in fifth grade, it has been my favorite unsolved mystery, hands down.

But my heart lay with true ghost stories. I could lose hours happily lost in a book, engrossed in tales of long-ago deaths whose repercussions were still being felt, of white figures drifting through the dusty halls of long-abandoned Southern mansions, of Spanish moss-draped trees standing silent guard over rows of marble tombstones. I grew up in the Chicago suburbs, hundreds of miles away from those haunted southern graveyards or western ghost towns, but we had our own ghostly infestations. My father thrilled me with stories of the ghostly monks of St.-James-the-Sag, the screaming mummy at the Field Museum, and the general weirdness of Archer Avenue. There was even a family story (that I heard only once, and have never been able to verify) that a buddy of a cousin of mine once gave a motorcycle ride to Resurrection Mary.

So when I grew up and started writing my own stories, to the surprise of absolutely no one, there were ghosts in them. I started writing spooky short stories, then graduated to horror novels. In fiction, I could keep the ghosts at arm's length. I could write about them, but they were safely on the page – and they certainly didn't affect me personally, except when I was through the rabbit hole and involved in writing the story.

Even when I became a paranormal investigator and wrote my first collection of true ghost stories – a childhood obsession brought to vital life – I was still a bit leery of really letting the spirits very far into my life. On learning that I am a ghost hunter, one of the questions I am routinely asked is, "Aren't you afraid that something will follow you home?" To that, I always give an honest reply.

"I don't think anything ever has. And even if something did follow me home from an investigation, it wouldn't stay more than a couple of weeks before getting bored to tears and leaving on its own. I'm not the least bit sensitive. Someone could be walking along behind me carrying their own severed head, and I wouldn't notice." This line invariably brings appreciative grimaces. And it happens to be true. I don't consider myself a sensitive – in fact, there have been several times where something paranormal has come up and pretty much smacked me in the face, and I've been oblivious until someone else pointed it out to me.

So since childhood, I've always been open to the idea of an invisible world of spirits coexisting alongside the living. But the actual existence of this world had always been ... academic.

Two things have happened to change that in the past several years.

I'm fortunate to live within a ten-minute motorcycle ride of an urban archaeology site right here in Illinois. If you go to Bartonville, turn west at the Illinois River and come up Pfeiffer Road, at the top of the hill you will see the Bowen Building, the nurses' dorm of the Peoria State Hospital. The building stares at you with blank eyes where her windows have been broken out. She sits at the top of the hill like a dead queen on a throne, garbed in robes of white limestone. You know she can't hurt you, but she is still sometimes kind of scary. Locally, the Peoria State Hospital was a magnet for urban exploration in the 1980s and 1990s. The asylum closed in 1973, and soon after that, the exploration began. Sometimes vandals ransacked the buildings, but more often, the secret midnight visitors were just kids, out to see what they could see in the abandoned cottages and steam tunnels. Some of them were pretty sure there were ghosts there too. And they were right.

When I was doing the research for my second nonfiction book, *Fractured Spirits: Hauntings at the Peoria State Hospital*, I spoke to many people who had some connection to the abandoned asylum. Some of them were nurses who had worked at the hospital when it was still open. Some were paranormal enthusiasts who had done investigations at the asylum, drawn by reports of ghostly activity. Some were just ordinary people with extraordinary stories to tell. No matter what their relation to the asylum was, I wanted to hear about their experiences. (That is, hands down, no exceptions, the very best part of doing what I do. I get to talk to all kinds of people, and I get to say, "Tell me stories!" And they do.)

One of the people I interviewed for *Fractured Spirits* was a medium who claimed she could see spirits. We were chatting at the Peoria Public Library on a bright summer day, with sunshine pouring in through the windows of the library atrium.

Even in that cheerful setting, the medium managed to send chills down my spine as she told of the lost souls she had encountered while taking a tour of the asylum cemeteries. (Her story of a young woman who kept repeating forlornly, "I shouldn't be here. I don't belong here," was particularly heartbreaking.)

At one point in our interview, the medium looked at me and told me, with a completely straight face, that my grandmother was near me much of the time. She described my Grandma Ruth accurately enough. I shifted uncomfortably on my stool "So she's around me, like, visiting?"

"Oh yes. In fact, she's standing behind you right now."

This was exactly the right thing to say to a fledgling ghost hunter – and a very disquieting thing to say to someone who hadn't yet conquered a lifelong fear of the dark. Some of my nervousness must have shown on my face, because the medium looked concerned – and a bit sorry she had shared the information. "Did you not get along well with your grandmother? Were you scared of her in life?"

"No! No, I adored her!" But believing academically that dead relatives are still with us, watching over us as we go about our lives, is one thing. Having someone tell you flat out that your favorite grandmother, who died when you were in your senior year of high school, is standing right behind you ... is something entirely different.

Since then, I have had plenty of people assure me that the spirit world is much closer than we think. I've had people tell me their stories of ghostly encounters, and I've had plenty of my own experiences. Fortunately, the spirits I hang out with in my volunteering at the Pollak Hospital have mostly been gentle souls. There seem to be several spirits that show up to hear my presentations about the history and hauntings at the Peoria State Hospital – sort of a spectral bunch of groupies. They can be playfully annoying at times, as when someone in the Women's Ward of the Pollak turned the lights off on me when I was sitting in the ward reading a book. They can be encouraging, like the nurse who showed up to a presentation, stood behind me the entire time I talked, and told a medium in the audience to tell me that "everyone on the Other Side is all atwitter that they're in a book." But for the most part, the spirits that I'm told are with me these days are gentle, pleasant entities.

Other people are not so lucky.

I first met Linda K. while I was doing research for *Fractured Spirits*. At the time, she was a member of Central Illinois Ghost Hunters – the founding member. She also had the gift of discernment and knowledge. She had been putting her gifts to good use as a paranormal investigator. I was thrilled to hear that CIGH had done an investigation at the Peoria State Hospital. I was looking forward to having her share her experiences with me.

For her interview in the summer of 2012, we met at the Cantina, a bar that my husband owned at the time. The Cantina also happened to be haunted, so after we chatted about the asylum, I invited Linda and her colleague Beth to walk through the bar to do their own impromptu daylight investigation. (Being at the bar several days a week, by the way, was the second of the two things I mentioned that radically changed my outlook on the world of spirits. The experiences I had in that building opened me once and for all to the reality that there is a world that exists side by side with our everyday life.)

There was a part of the building, a small hallway between the front room and the office, that always made people with any amount of sensitivity uncomfortable. Heck, I even felt weird back there, and I'm about as sensitive as a dining room table. It was Linda who was able to describe for me why people – especially women – feel inexplicably depressed in that short hallway.

"There's a woman here. She's having an affair, and her husband just found out." Linda's voice was somber. "He's just caught them together. There was a fight…"

I could almost hear the woman crying, pulling at her husband's arm to keep him from hitting her lover one more time. I could nearly see a man lying on the floor, blood dripping from his smashed nose onto the cracked tiles, his teeth bloody as he snarled up at his rival.

Several months later, CIGH came to the bar for a proper investigation. A medium who worked with the group – not Linda – told us her impressions of the office. "There's a woman in here. She's inexpressibly sad over the fight between her husband and the guy she was seeing behind his back. She's sitting on the bed … every so often she gets up and goes to look out the window, but she's mostly sitting on the bed, too depressed to move." The medium was referring, of course, to a bed that had been in that room decades before, when the argument took place. "I'm trying to get her to talk to me. I'm trying to tell her everything's okay now, but she's just ignoring me." This spirit seemed to be one of several "recording" hauntings at the bar.

Linda, Beth, and I came through the hallway into the front room. In front of the beautiful bay windows that look out onto Court Street, we bowed our heads, and Linda spoke to the woman, encouraging her to go to the Light. We said the Lord's Prayer, and Linda seemed satisfied that she had helped the entity. As someone who had a deep connection to the bar, I was impressed with the compassionate way Linda approached the spirits in the building. I was especially glad of the gentle way she talked with the distraught woman, an earthbound spirit who so badly wanted to be free.

I don't know if that woman's spirit went to the Light, as Linda had invited her to do. She still seemed to be tied to the building, mired in her sorrow, months later during the other investigation.

What I do know is this: Linda had a small recorder with her that day, and it ran for the entire time we were walking around the bar. As I showed Linda and Beth to the door, the recorder was still running. A few days after our meeting, Linda sent me an EVP that had shown up on the device as we stood at the top of the stairs saying our goodbyes.

A woman's clear voice softly says, "*Thank you, Linda.*"

Linda and I exchanged a few emails over the next couple of years. Her group, CIGH, came to do a nighttime investigation of the bar, but Linda wasn't with them. I didn't see her again until the winter of 2014.

The library at which I work moved to a new building late in 2013. The library had been open only a few months when Linda came in to see me.

She was the same gentle, peaceful soul I remembered from our meeting the summer before. And yet, there was something indefinably different about her – some deep knowledge hidden in her eyes. We exchanged hellos, and made small talk for a few minutes. Then she hesitated, and asked if there was somewhere more private, where we could talk for a bit.

I took her over to the book sale corner, several yards away from the bustle of the circulation desk. In the relative quiet of the corner, she turned to face me. The tale she told me then raised some serious goosebumps on my arms.

"You know how the Bible says we fight not against flesh and blood, but against spiritual beings? It's true, it's so absolutely true. I want people to know about this. I have a story, and I want you to help me tell it."

I listened to her story. What else could I do? And what I heard would forever change the way I felt about ghosts, and spirituality, and the world that coexists with ours, unseen, but as close to us as our own heartbeats.

2. INTO THE FIELD: A LOOK AT GHOST HUNTING

Ghost hunting is a lot like deer hunting, and yes, I've done both. They both involve specialized equipment, and some advance preparation. First comes the scouting part. You walk through the woods, quietly looking for the best location for your tree stand. It has to be in a place where there's likely to be action – say, at a buck scrape, or along a well-travelled deer path. It's just like going through a haunted location with an EMF meter, eliminating sources of electrical power so as not to mistake them for paranormal activity. You also want to find out where the best spots are, the spots at which you're most likely to witness activity. You get into position – and then it's lots of waiting around, hours sometimes, for something to happen. Your ears strain to hear footsteps, a voice, any sort of noise to let the hunter know the prey is near. If you're lucky, something happens, and you come home in triumph to fill your freezer with venison – or your computer with EVPs and photographs.

Out in the woods, beyond the safe circle of the firelight, there are other animals – predators, not prey. The tiger sleeps soundly at night because she is an apex predator. What are we hunting, with our night-vision cameras and our MEL meters and our spirit boxes?

Are we hunting gazelles ... or tigers?

Ghosts have been around since cavemen smeared the bodies of the dead with red ochre to symbolize the blood of birth, and tucked the handle of a favorite knife or a hide scraper into a lifeless hand. Ghosts have prowled the shafts of the Great Pyramid and the chambers of the Valley of the Kings. They have stalked the Hanging Gardens of Babylon and the halls of China's Forbidden City. They have muttered and moaned along Rome's Appian Way, the street outside the city limits lined with cemeteries.

Ancient Egyptians recognized demons, too. Illness was considered a demonic being all on its own, with its own personality. An exorcism has come down to us all these centuries later, an incantation against childhood disease. "Go hence, thou who comest in darkness, whose nose is turned backwards, whose face is upside down and who knowest not why thou hast come. Hast thou come to kiss this child? I will not let thee kiss him. Hast thou come to send him to sleep? I will not let thee do him harm. Hast thou come to take him with thee? I will not let thee carry him away."

The Roman historian Pliny the Younger told the story of the philosopher Athenodorus, who spent the night in a haunted house. The house was haunted by a spectre who would appear at midnight, rattling chains and moaning horribly. The ghost was so frightening, in fact, that the previous owners had simply died of fright and stress. Athenodorus saw the cheap price of the house, and asked about it. Even after hearing the story, he couldn't pass up a bargain, so he bought the house. That night, he had a table set up with his writing materials, then sent his servants away for the evening. He sat down to write, and several hours passed uneventfully. But at midnight, the emaciated phantom showed up, rattling its chains to get the philosopher's attention. Athenodorus held up a finger, and motioned to the ghost to wait until he'd finished jotting down his sentence. The ghost moaned and rattled its chains insistently. Finally, Athenodorus put his pen down, got up from his chair, and followed the beckoning spirit. The ghost led him to another part of the house, where it suddenly vanished. Athenodorus piled a small handful of leaves and twigs at the spot, then went off to bed. The next day, he contacted the magistrate, and together they dug at the spot where the ghost had vanished. A skeleton was found, bound in chains. The magistrate collected the bones, and Athenodorus paid for a funeral. The ghost was finally laid to rest.

Ghosts have been rattling around European castles for centuries. And they've survived the passage of the years. The Tower of London is still home to the restless spirit of Anne Boleyn, with "her head tucked underneath her arm," and those of so many others who met their fate within those chilling stone walls.

In the late 1800s, America got very interested in ghosts and the supernatural. Interest in the occult and spiritual matters evolved through the Spiritualist movement after the Civil War, on into the Occult Revival.

The Spiritualist movement grew out of the terror and grief of the Civil War. Families of soldiers killed on the battlefields were desperate for any sign of their loved ones' survival beyond the Veil. Grieving families, including the quintessential widow, Mary Todd Lincoln, held séances in a bid to contact the souls of those who had been taken from them so unfairly.

During the Occult Revival of the late 1800s, many intellectuals, writers, and artists joined magickal fraternities and dabbled in psychic research (or threw themselves into it wholeheartedly). Harry Houdini, who has since become the poster child for attempts at communication from beyond the grave, visited many mediums in the hopes of getting in touch with his dead mother. As a result of his search, Houdini developed a keen eye for fraud and chicanery in the swirling shadows of the séance parlor.

On October 6, 2004, paranormal seekers everywhere got their first fix of exploring haunted places while sitting in the comfort of their own living rooms. *Ghost Hunters* featured a pair of plumbers turned paranormal investigators, Jason Hawes and Grant Wilson. Their ghost hunting group, The Atlantic Paranormal Society (TAPS), went to haunted places and did paranormal investigations – and filmed them for the viewing public. And the viewing public ate it up. People who wouldn't dream of wandering through a cemetery at night, or sitting in a spooky attic asking questions of a ghost, were suddenly able to watch someone else doing these scary things. And the best part about it was that the audience didn't have to sit through hours of nothing happening, the way investigators in real life often do. Hawes and Wilson were quick to admit that most of their investigations, just like ghost hunts in the real world, have very little activity. What audiences saw were the really spectacular parts – the shadow people, the glowing mists, anything creepy the crew happened to catch on film.

The next big show to come along tried to scare up more great moments for their audiences. Zak Bagans, Nick Groff, and Aaron Goodwin, the crew of *Ghost Adventures*, are known for their more aggressive ghost hunting techniques. They have themselves locked inside their site for the entire night. If you're going to be at a site, you might as well be there for the duration. And the longer you're there, the more likely it is that something will happen. (And hopefully, again, you'll catch it on tape.) The Ghost Adventures crew is often accused of provoking the spirits, which some ghost hunters feel is, well, rude. You don't go into someone's home for a visit and start casing on them. But Groff has defended the practice, saying that it stirs up energy for the spirits to use to manifest.

Across the pond, where ghosts have been hanging out for centuries, the British ghost hunting show *Most Haunted* first aired on May 25, 2002. This show takes a more measured approach to ghost hunting. Their shows feature a main presenter, who is accompanied by a historian, a psychic medium, and a parapsychologist. The idea is to strike a balance between the paranormal and scientific explanations.

All of these shows, serious or playful, those that provoke our imaginations and those that just provoke, suffer from one unavoidable flaw. None of them reflect the reality of ghost hunting – and they can't, not really. A network would never go for it.

People – especially paranormal investigators – take a perverse pleasure in pointing out that ghost hunting reality shows are nothing like actual investigations. Well, of course they aren't. Actual investigations can last six hours or more. Most of an investigation consists of sitting around waiting for something to happen. And I'm not even including time for setting up all the cool equipment at the beginning of the evening, and tearing it down at the end. Even if you're just wandering around a cemetery with nothing more than a recorder and the camera on your cell phone, it still takes up time. A show like *Ghost Hunters* is, of necessity, composed of only the most exciting moments.

Most paranormal shows aren't running into demons around every corner, either. For that, popular culture has an entire channel-surfing, popcorn-munching lineup of horror shows. Movies about demons abound, too, from *The Rite, The Unborn, and The Exorcist* all the way to *Oh God! You Devil* and *Little Nicky*. There is even – and I am not making this up – a movie called *Shark Exorcist*. Really. A demonic nun summons the Devil to possess a man-eating shark, that then starts chowing down on a lot of girls in bikinis. Some of these movies are serious when it comes to their scares. Some are just in it for the laughs. But all of them, whether silly or serious, use demons as their main characters.

For my money, the most gonzo of these shows when it comes to demons is the enormously popular *Supernatural*. The demons on this show follow many of the rules – as far as preternatural creatures can follow rules – as demons do in real life. They cringe and smoke when spattered with holy water, they hang around in a telltale funk of sulfur, treat their human hosts with casual cruelty, referring to them contemptuously as "meat suits". When the writers of the show want to reveal without a doubt that a new character is a demon in human disguise, the CGI artists give the actor inky-black eyes. This fits with the lore. Not only have exorcists reported that possessed people's eyes roll back in their heads, showing only the whites, they also report possessions in which the victim's eyes momentarily flash completely black – iris, sclera, and all. The demons on Supernatural can be summoned, many times at a crossroads, with sigils and spells, and they can be repelled – or contained – with blessed salt.

Most tellingly, the demons of the *Supernatural* universe have free will, just like humans do. Just as in our own world, angels on *Supernatural* were created to adore God. The angels that fell from grace, though, were endowed with free will. Humans, too, have free will – the idea being that humans can choose on their own to worship God. After all, love is most precious if it's freely given.

The lore of *Supernatural* is thorough in its depiction of demons. They show up many times during a season, especially the closer we get to a season finale. Ghost hunting shows, on the other hand, can go entire seasons without running into any spirits that are even remotely demonic. And the heroic team of Sam and Dean Winchester are coolly competent in their handling of any demonic situation. They can summon and bind demons with ease, and they fight the good fight with holy water and Latin incantations. Of course, the heroes have to be smarter than the demons. They also have to best the demons within the time constraints of a one-hour show. What if – and here's a thought – what if the sensational, far-out, crazy horror fiction show is more accurate in its description of the infernal than the ghost hunting reality shows are?

What if Dean Winchester is better at his job than Zak Bagans is?

In a 2004 Gallup poll, about 70% of Americans reported that they believe in the Devil, with a capital D. Many more people believe in demons in general, as well as angels. And many of those feel that that they are plagued by those spirits. According to the Association of Italian Catholic Psychiatrists and Psychologists, more than half a million people in Italy alone see an exorcist every year to find relief from their demons.

Another poll, this one by YouGov, got even more detailed: 57% of people polled said that the Devil exists. Of these respondents, 72% were black, 61% were women, and 65% were Republican. There weren't as many believers among better-educated respondents. The poll noted that 63% of people with a high school education said they believe in Satan, compared to 48% of college graduates. Regionally, most believers live in the South. It noted that 64% of Southerners fear the Devil compared to 56% in the Midwest, 52% in the West, and 48% in the Northeast. Four in ten respondents believed that people can occasionally be possessed by the Devil, with 46% believing in the power of exorcism. Only one in ten said Satan never possessed humans. Most believers in the Devil (86%) were affiliated with Christianity in general, over Catholicism (66%), Judaism (17%), and Islam (25%).

Many priests, though, struggle with the concept of evil. For some, evil is an abstract concept, more of a falling away from God than an active intent. But just as day and night are two sides of the same twenty-four hours, just as death follows life and spring follows winter, good can't exist without evil.

3. HOW DID WE GET HERE, ANYWAY?

Humans have ached for a communication with the divine from the very earliest morning twilight of our being. It's why we braved cave bears and sudden drop offs and the pitch blackness of the depths of the earth to make our marks, slapping sooty, fevered hands on cold damp walls. Religion could also have been an evolutionary advantage for early man. A deer hunter, for example, focused on the idea of his prey, even as he stalked it. Pushing himself to the limits of his endurance, trekking for miles across the landscape, battling hunger and little sleep, this hunter held in his mind an image of perfection, a Great Stag. In the theater of his imagination, he pictured an animal big enough to feed himself and his family, saving them from starvation. Then, when the hunter finally came across a real deer, the prey was seen as a gift from this divine Great Stag. The first primal gods developed from the imaginations of the hunters who went out to battle the elements and track prey to feed their families.

Religion evolved over many thousands of years, from the animal spirits depicted on cave walls, to the animal-headed gods of the ancient Egyptians. These human-animal hybrids became the fully human-looking divinities of Greece and Rome, gods and goddesses who were divine, but had human appetites and flaws.

The Greek gods, for example, definitely had their good days and their bad days. The gods were seen as divine, but not remote. And they absolutely had their own personalities. Zeus was always throwing lightning bolts, Hera was constantly getting into pissy moods (usually after catching her husband Zeus in one of his many infidelities), and Aphrodite, the goddess of love and beauty, could be as vain and flighty as any reality TV star. Even patient Athena could take offense if a mortal got uppity with her. Poor Arachne dared to compare her skill at weaving to that of the goddess, and Athena turned her into a spider to punish her.

The religions of Judaism and Christianity went the classical world one better, and decided that God *is* human. The Judeo-Christian God loved humanity so much, He sent his son to become human and walk among His creations. When it comes to religion, God-as-human is about as personal as you can get.

Our ancestors may have been primitive, but they certainly weren't stupid. They knew about the movements of the stars and the planets. They kept track of the changing seasons – they had to, much more than we do today. Successful agriculture depended on it.

They also had a grasp of more esoteric things – language, philosophy, thoughts, symbols, and ideas. But until the Age of Reason and the scientific revolution, people didn't have a frame of reference to separate these fuzzier concepts from the workaday world of reality. When the distinction between the physical world and the world of symbols is blurred, there is room in that blurriness for magical thinking and for nonhuman entities.

In the Middle Ages, the whole world was like this – magical. There was a direct link between symbolism and the physical structure of things. An obvious example of this is the belief, which continued up through the Salem Witch Trials, that a person could affect another person's life by making a doll. Injury to the doll would result in injury to the person in whose image the doll was made. People in the Middle Ages truly believed that "storm makers" could whip up a storm out of nowhere, just by swishing a stick in a puddle of water. Medieval people lived in constant fear of harmful magic.

This saturation of magic in the world meant that daily life was an incredibly busy place. People shared their world with a dizzying array of nonhuman beings – fairies, sprites, leprechauns, talking animals, spirits of fountains and trees. All of these creatures were seen as having their own personalities, neither good nor evil, much like humans.

In medieval Europe, the main nonhuman entities were grouped into three categories: angels, demons, and saints. Angels, being closer to God, were naturally well above matters of petty humanity. But demons and saints were pretty thick on the ground. They played their roles in the daily life of every noble and peasant.

Demons were ever-present, and very dangerous. One of the most famous medieval authors on demons was the German monk Caesarius of Heisterbach (died 1240). He collected many stories in which demons attacked humans. People fell sick or even died just from seeing a demon, in these accounts. One of the monk's stories concerned a soldier who spent all night playing cards with a demon, then was found the next morning with his entrails torn out.

Demons also had the job of leading the faithful away from God and into sin. Medieval people always had to be on their guard. According to the Church, demons were always waiting to lure people into sin, especially sins of the flesh. The church warned against having sex with demons and the risk that a woman might as a result give birth to a monster.

Luckily for everyone, though, there were also saints. Demons hated saints, and were terrified of them. Exorcising demons and chasing them away was standard in most every saint's repertoire.

Saint Anthony (251-356), a desert-dwelling monk, was a wealth of knowledge on the subject of demons. He was harassed by demons throughout most of his life, and spent a lot of his time pondering the nature of his attackers. He wrote that demons were not originally evil. He pointed out that God made nothing evil, therefore demons had started out as good. "Having fallen, however, from the heavenly wisdom, since then they have been groveling on earth." Christians should not fear demons, Anthony said, because demons are liars and cowards. They threaten and bluster, but they have no real power to carry out those threats.

Anthony gained great renown as an exorcist. People would seek out the desert tomb where he lived in isolation, and bang on his door, begging for help. Sometimes, Anthony wouldn't answer, leaving the afflicted person to camp out on his doorstep. Often they would be healed just because they had stayed and kept up a prayerful vigil at the door of Anthony's cell.

Saints regularly kept the populace safe from demons not only during their lifetimes, but also well after death. Even the tiniest relic of a saint, a finger bone or a lock of hair, was powerful enough to banish demons.

This familiarity with the invisible wasn't necessarily something negative. Sure, demons and harmful magic could be scary. But on the other hand, the protection of saints and the use of household charms were simply means to make life easier. Before the Inquisition, when people were brought to trial for witchcraft or other harmful magic, they were simply on trial for damage to another person or their property. A witchcraft trial was a criminal matter, not a spiritual one.

Even the Church got into the spirit of things. Medieval church artists forged an alliance with symbols of the demonic. Cathedrals bristled with gargoyles, their fierce faces grimacing with menace. The message was written in stone for any passing demon to read: "There's no room for you here. Go find somewhere else to hang around. We're full up with demons already, as you can see, so move along."

During the Middle Ages, things really started to ramp up as far as Western thought and philosophy went. Social life settled down around the year 1000. The barbarian hordes had finished breaking up the Roman Empire by that time, so when the dust had settled from that, people were able to catch their breath. They settled down and formed cities, and by 1200 or so, universities had sprung up in places like Paris, Bologne, and Oxford. With this new age of peace and stability, the time was ripe for a revolution in quiet thought. This particular intellectual revolution was known as scholasticism.

Scholasticism brought about a shift in attitude, from seeing the universe as governed by personalities (gods, angels, demons) to a view of the universe as governed by physical laws. In early medieval thought, the world was the stage for struggles between personalities – God versus Satan, kings versus commoners, demons versus saints. People also had their own struggles with demons, or had help from saints.

With this new era of thought, however, the scholastics turned back to the philosophy of Aristotle. They suggested that the universe could be understood on the basis of natural laws, not spiritual personalities. This led to a split between the physical world and the spiritual world. Thinkers like Thomas Aquinas (1225-1274) reasoned that demons and angels were purely spiritual beings. Therefore, they couldn't share the physical world with humans. And that meant that humans were incapable of causing physical events to happen simply by using symbolic actions. So if someone practiced sympathetic magic, whether helpful or harmful, if that magic turned out to have a physical effect, it was because it was helped along by demons. According to this new way of thought, in this law-ordered universe, to dabble in magic was not only to seek help from demons, it also meant tampering with the order of the cosmos.

During the next two hundred years, cities continued to expand, and universities became well-respected bulwarks of learning. Smaller colleges joined them, as the intellectual life outgrew the walls of monasteries and joined the mainstream. The Renaissance was the time of da Vinci, Galileo, Michelangelo, and other giants of intellect.

But there was a problem – a serious one. These enlightened thinkers of the Renaissance were surrounded by the masses of the common people, who were still living in the Dark Ages. The vast majority of the population was not strolling around ivy-covered university campuses thinking Great Thoughts. They were still living life using a combination of Christianity and pagan magic, with the attitude of "if it ain't broke, don't fix it". Most of the populace was still putting out bread and milk for their garden gnomes, and throwing salt over their left shoulder into the Devil's eye if they spilled any. They happily made offerings, trusting that the gnomes would keep the Fair Folk out of the garden. Fairies were unpredictable and dangerous – much better to have a gnome around the place than have it infested with fairies. But gnomes could be dangerous too. If you forgot to pour fresh cream over the porridge offering, there was a good chance the gnome would take offense and kill your livestock in a fit of pique. They believed in the reality of ghosts, goblins, saints, demons, and other supernatural beings.

This freaked out the intellectuals. They were living in a philosophically and spiritually precarious time in history. They saw everyone around them casually practicing magic, which the thinkers saw as not only unnatural, but actively sinful. But the Scientific Revolution was still several centuries away, and these intellectuals didn't yet have scientific advances to back up their "laws of the universe" theories. The science of the time just wasn't enough to disprove the reality of magic. Furthermore, many of these revolutionary thinkers had childhood memories themselves of magical practices.

This created a panic among the intellectual elite. The more they became convinced that the world worked in a scientific manner, the more threatening the magical practices of the common folk seemed to them. The more the Renaissance expanded, and the more logical thought became entrenched, the more this intellectual panic increased. The thinkers tried frantically to come up with some interpretation for this behavior that was causing them such mental anguish.

They came up with the Witches' Sabbath.

The Witches' Sabbath was the idea that marked the beginning of the great European witch hunt. Heretics were accused of making pacts with the Devil and getting up to all sorts of shenanigans, including flying between villages at night to meet with their co-conspirators, killing and eating children (their own and other people's), and having sex with demons. The accused were mostly women, and they were further accused of having babies just for the sake of sacrificing them to Satan.

Historian Norman Cohn notes that some people, again, mostly women, went to the authorities and voluntarily confessed to these crimes, including cannibalism and infanticide. Of course, these confessions just gave the inquisitors more evidence. He wrote:

"It seems ... that ecclesiastical and secular authorities alike ... repeatedly came across people – chiefly women – who believed things about themselves which fitted perfectly with the tales about heretical sects that had been circulating for centuries. The notion of cannibalistic infanticide provided the common factor. It was widely believed that babies or small children were devoured at the nocturnal meetings of heretics. It was likewise widely believed that certain women killed or devoured babies or small children; also at night; and some women even believed this of themselves. It was the extraordinary congruence between the two sets of beliefs that led those concerned with pursuing heretics to see, in the stories which they extracted from deluded women, a confirmation of the traditional stories about heretics who practiced cannibalistic infanticide."

These voluntary confessions have a disturbing parallel in today's world: they closely resemble claims made by women who suffer from Multiple Personality Disorder. The women of the 14th century, who were convinced that they had had sex with demons, had given birth, and then had sacrificed their own children, may have been suffering from the same disorder.

On December 5, 1484, Pope Innocent VIII issued a papal edict sanctioning action against suspected witches. The church members who took it upon themselves to go out and find these witches were called Inquisitors. And boy, did they take their job seriously. In 1487, Jakob Sprenger and Heinrich Kramer published the *Malleus Maleficarum*, known in English as *The Witch's Hammer*. This was a manual for witch hunters, part scripture, part encyclopedia, all vicious. Heinrich Kramer wrote the book after being kicked out of the church at Innsbruck by the local bishop after a failed attempt to conduct his own witch trials. Kramer had several goals in writing the *Malleus Maleficarum*. He wanted magistrates to use his witch-hunting techniques, of course. He also intended to convince people that witchcraft did exist, and that those who practiced it were more often women than men.

Lurid stories of witchcraft – and worse – were also splashed across the headlines of the broadsheets of the day. In 1591, a German publisher named Georg Kress spread the "horrifying and never before heard" news that 300 female werewolves had been on the loose in the Duchy of Julich. These women, it was said, had made a pact with the Devil that allowed them to turn into wolves. They attacked men, boys, and cattle, slaughtering them while in wolf form. The broadsheet reported the relieving news that 85 of the women were caught and burned at the stake on May 6, 1591.

Hannah Priest, editor of *She-Wolf: A Cultural History of Female Werewolves* (Manchester University Press, 2015) writes, "Perhaps partly a response to the anxieties engendered by both the Inquisition and the Reformation, a growing taste for lurid and bloodthirsty 'news' encouraged publishers to churn out increasingly fantastical tales of diabolical individuals, causing a dramatic rise in such stories at the end of the 16th century." The story of the She-Wolves of Julich is one of those sweaty, hyperbolic fantasies. And it was, of course, blown ludicrously out of proportion for the benefit of Kress' readers. The "300 women" of the blaring headline is a bit of an exaggeration, since the actual story involves … one woman. And the part about 85 women being burned at the stake is a stretch too. The text only says that the arrested woman implicated 24 others. That's it. But Kress was giving his readers what they wanted.

This paranoid line of thinking continued all the way up until the Salem Witch Trials, even crossing the Atlantic with the Puritans. Puritan doctrine forbade the use of magic, of course, but not every colonist was Puritan. Even those who were believers probably didn't understand the finer points of theology. Magic was used to solve many of the niggling problems of daily life. The use of charms, counter-spells, astrology, and other hearth magic was popular and widespread.

Cotton Mather, the driving force behind the trials, had a personal horror of demons that bordered on the pathological. An overachiever who entered Harvard at age twelve, he was already so fluent in Latin that he could take notes in Latin on a sermon being preached in English. He could also read Greek, and two years later could write Hebrew.

Mather went through life keenly aware of the burden he carried just by virtue of his name. He was named after his two grandfathers, John Cotton and Richard Mather – who happened to be two of the religious founders of the colony. Cotton's father, Increase Mather, was the president of Harvard and also penned many religious books. Not only was Cotton Mather stuck with this daunting heritage to live up to, he was a staunch Puritan himself.

Puritanism focused on the innate helplessness and sinfulness of humankind. It was a very austere, unforgiving religion, a source of anxiety and stress even for those in the colony who were among the less pious. For Cotton Mather, this severity of thought ate at him for his entire life.

To add to this stress, Mather's generation was firmly entrenched in the colony. The first generation to colonize Massachusetts had survived, and now this generation was prospering in the New World. The preachers, Mather among them, feared that the faithful were growing complacent, and that Puritanism as they knew it was dying out. They felt that the focus of the people was shifting from religious idealism to more worldly concerns. Now that the survival of the colony was safely assured, it was time to think about creature comforts. Cotton Mather brooded over this heresy. The anxiety he felt over the state of his own soul was magnified by the degeneration he saw surrounding him.

Cotton Mather – and his victims – had the unfortunate distinction of living in yet another one of those paradigm shifts of history. The Age of Reason was just beginning. In one short generation, people would come to see witchcraft as hopelessly backwards, and to interpret the world through the lens of science. Just as the Renaissance shifted thought from a symbolic worldview to one of natural law, the 1700s moved the perception of the world even closer to rational thought. The universe would come to be seen as a sort of perpetual-motion machine, rather than a place of mystery peopled by invisible beings. In this interpretation, there was absolutely no room for the mystical.

Cotton Mather was educated in the 1670s, so he knew about the scientific revolution. But his outlook on life was much closer to the Middle Ages than to the Age of Reason. This made him more than a little fanatic when it came to putting someone on trial for witchcraft.

One of the voices of reason in the witch trials was Major Robert Pike. He was a magistrate who collected the depositions used in the trials. Pike was quite concerned about "spectral evidence," or the idea that the Devil could appear to accused witches. Like all good Puritans who were steeped in Old Testament teachings, Pike knew the story of the Witch of Endor, how she used necromancy to call up the Devil – but that the Devil had appeared using the form of Samuel, the revered prophet. This seemed to throw a wrench into the works. If the Devil could appear as a trusted guide, who could people then trust?

Pike also pointed out to Jonathan Corwin, another witch trials judge, that it made no sense for the accused witches to use their powers against the afflicted in the courtroom, thus proving their own guilt. Similarly, why would the Devil urge the accused to confess, and to point out others who had signed his pact? That made no sense, unless, as Pike said, "the Devil hath changed his nature, and is now become a reformer to purge witches out of the world, out of the country, and out of the churches; and is to be believed, though [he is] a liar and a murderer from the beginning."

The magistrates and government officials in Massachusetts had a fine line to walk both during and after the witch trials. While even some educated people still believed that witches were real, most people were coming to the conclusion that innocent people had been condemned to death. These were friends, neighbors, fellow church members. And they were gone.

According to Puritan belief, anyone who committed a sin must confess it before God. And if the courts had put people to death unfairly, that was murder. That should have been acknowledged publicly – and failing to do so jeopardized the well-being of the colony and the foundations of the Puritans' special covenant with God.

The colony was already suffering. By 1696, people were already looking back with real regret on the sorry business of 1692, feeling that the colony was being punished for its reckless execution of twenty people and the unfair imprisonment of dozens more. King William's War – the first of what would later be known as the French and Indian Wars – was still raging. The spring of 1696 brought famine in the form of a killing frost that wiped out the young corn. Unseasonably cold weather further delayed planting, and the price of corn doubled. By December of that year, the colony was in serious trouble, with severe food shortages, and the worst winter since the English had settled in Massachusetts.

But making it right had other consequences. If the government of the colony admitted to the wrongful death or imprisonment of more than 150 innocent citizens, it would lose all sense of authority. So Governor Phips and Cotton Mather decided to suppress the truth. Mather wrote a book about the trials, defending the actions of the judges. Then Phips banned the publication of any further discussion.

The Salem Witch Trials turned out to be not only a religious crisis, but a political crisis as well. We tend to see the trials, from the distance of four centuries, as being almost purely religious, "Puritans versus nonconformists." But there was so much more going on, other factors that affected the situation. The trials were the culmination of centuries of scholarship and debate. This was a chance for a real change in the way the authorities looked at religion, at God and the Devil, and in the way they interpreted the behavior of those who dared to behave a little differently.

It was a start, but it was Vatican II that really shook things up. Vatican II was the second council to be held at St. Peter's Basilica in the Vatican in Rome. (It was actually the twenty-first ecumenical council held by the Catholic Church.) It opened on October 11, 1962, when John XXIII was pope, and closed under Pope Paul VI in 1965.

Vatican II was unique in that it didn't issue new dogmas or resolve grave heresies. Instead, its purpose was to renew and refine Catholic doctrine, bringing it into the modern world. The Church, and especially the Mass, underwent several marked changes as a result. Most of these changes had to do with making the Church more accessible to the congregations. Priests who had previously intoned the mass in Latin now spoke it in English (or in the language of whatever country they were celebrating in). Priests also faced the congregation to say Mass, instead of facing East towards the Lord (which often put their backs to the people). Priestly regalia and church artwork also became less ornate. (I was raised in the Orthodox Church, but I went to a Catholic school for several years. I've been to plenty of masses and liturgies in both churches. There is a world of difference between the intense colors, gold and incense of an Orthodox liturgy and the fresh, streamlined decoration of a Catholic church.)

The position of the Church had always been that Satan and his fallen angels were created beings. Lucifer had been the Light Bearer, one of God's trusted angels, but had been cast out of Heaven, taking a third of the angels with him.

But with the Second Vatican Council, the Catholic Church took a good hard look at the nearly two millennia of its history, and decided that it was time for radical change. Along with the loosening of the rigid rules of centuries came a new way of looking at all the old beliefs. One of the questions that divided liberal and conservative theologians was whether the Devil was a concept that should be interpreted literally. Conservatives pointed out that every Christian was expected to cast out demons – Jesus specifically gave them permission to do so. If Jesus believed in the Devil and in demons, then his followers ought to believe too.

But liberal theologians analyzed those very same Bible passages, and pointed to their use of allegory to explain evil. After all, they said, it was rather backward and old-fashioned to believe in things like Satan and other "unclean spirits" in these modern times. Diseases weren't caused by bad air or curses, they were caused by germs, which could be combatted by hand washing and antibiotics. The theologian Rudolf Bultmann, writing in 1969, put it bluntly: "We cannot use electric light and radio, or turn to modern medicine in cases of sickness, and at the same time believe in a spirit world and in the miracles that the New Testament presents us." In other words, get out of the Dark Ages and join the twentieth century.

The Second Vatican Council aimed to open up the Church to the light of modern times, and sweep away centuries of dusty superstitions. For many Christians, priests and parishioners alike, this attitude is what has led them into the brave new world of the 21st century. The Devil became one of those superstitions, a relic of the olden days that no modern priest would dignify with attention.

4. DEMONS IN THE NEW WORLD: THE AMERICAN EXPERIENCE

Americans have always had a unique and rather personal relationship with the demonic. When Europeans got to the New World, they had no idea how huge and how frightening it could be. Everywhere they looked, all they could see was darkness, trees, and savages. The New World was a massive continent of the unknown stretching out before them.

So the earliest colonists, god-fearing, upright Christians that they were, named the places of their terrifying new home after that most terrifying of creatures, the Devil. This nod to the wildness of the North American continent continued as the new nation pushed the frontier westward. Devil's Windpipe. Satan Pass. Devil's Den Canyon. Devil's Chimney. Route 666. Devil's Bathtub. Devil's Darning Needle

Hollow. Hellfire Run. Dirty Devil River. Any place that pioneers found treacherous, ominous, or just plain weird, had a Satanic name slapped on it.

A designer named Jonathan Hull actually made a map of all the place names in the United States that mention "Devil" and "Hell", with a few variations. If he had included every place name with infernal connotations, the map would have been much more extensive.

Before the Westward Expansion, though, before the relentless push to the Pacific, before the colonists kicked over British traces – twice – there was the holy terror of the Salem Witch Trials.

The trouble started early in 1692. In January, there was a commotion at the house of the Reverend Samuel Parris in Salem Village, Massachusetts. Parris' niece, Abigail Williams, and his daughter, Betty Parris, began to suffer from fits. In February, a homeless woman named Sarah Good came to the door of the Parris house, begging for food for her baby and her four year old daughter, Dorcas. The girls' fits continued, and Samuel Parris was desperate to find the cause behind them. Under questioning, the girls revealed a terrible secret – it was witchcraft. They named Tituba, the Parris' Indian slave, as one of their tormentors. After all, no one trusted those pagan Indians. The other witch named was Sarah Good. After all, no one trusted a homeless smelly beggar woman. The girls also named the bedridden Sarah Osborn, who had not gone to church for over a year. On February 29, 1692, Tituba, Good, and Osborn were arrested, and the farce began.

The accusations continued to fly all throughout the rest of the winter, on into spring. By late April, the plague had spread from Salem Village to thirty-four of the surrounding towns. Between May 2 and June 6, thirty-nine more people were charged with witchcraft. Not all of these witches were even human. Two dogs were accused of being able to cause fits just by staring at their victims. They were hanged without benefit of trial.

The accused included Goodwife Rebecca Nurse, 71 years old, well-respected in the community, and sick in bed when she was fingered as a witch. They included George Jacobs Sr., the grandfather of Margaret Jacobs. Margaret was being questioned by the magistrates when she suddenly confessed to being a witch, and accused her grandfather of being a wizard. At that time, George Jacobs Sr. was a toothless old man of eighty, suffering terribly with rheumatism, who could get around only with the help of two walking sticks. When he was asked by the magistrates why his household did not pray from the Bible, he tartly replied, "I cannot read." They included Martha and Giles Cory. Martha was one of the Puritan elect, a Gospel Woman, a well-regarded member of the church. She made the mistake of telling her neighbors that she thought the witchcraft accusations were a lot of nonsense. Giles was another eighty year old farmer, a crusty, cantankerous fellow who cared nothing for public opinion. They included Bridget Bishop, the proprietress of a rowdy tavern, who had never even been to Salem Village.

By May, the jails were crammed full of people that had been accused. On May 14, Governor William Phips arrived back in Massachusetts from a visit to London. He immediately asked his council to nominate new judges to serve in a Court of Oyer and Terminer (meaning "hear and determine"). Not one of the judges nominated had ever served in a court of law. The few trained lawyers who had been practicing in the Massachusetts Bay Colony had been educated in England, and had gotten so disgusted with the process of law in the colony that they'd thrown up their hands and gone back home. The first lawyer educated in America, at Harvard, wouldn't even be admitted to the college until October 18, 1692, five months in the future. Needing to get the wheels of justice turning, Governor Phips approved the nominations quickly, and on May 27, the hearings began.

All of the people who were in jail awaiting trial had been accused by the use of "spectral evidence," a legal term referring to evidence relating to supernatural beings who were invisible to everyone except for the afflicted accusers. Hardly any evidence came from the natural world, the world of the five senses, of things people could normally touch and hear and see.

The first to be tried was Bridget Bishop. She was also the first to be hanged, on June 10. Five days after the hanging, a judge named Nathaniel Saltonstall resigned from the Court of Oyer and Terminer in disgust. That same day, fourteen ministers from twelve different towns presented a message to the court. Written by Cotton Mather, with a nudge from Major Robert Pike, it said that spectral evidence should never be used all by itself in court, but must be accompanied by natural evidence. The court ignored the missive, and soon after that, Judge Saltonstall himself was accused of being a witch.

The last eight victims were hanged on Gallows Hill on September 22. In all, nineteen people were hanged as witches, and one, Giles Cory, was pressed to death under rocks. It was Cory's horrible death that increased public opposition to the trials.

On October 3, Increase Mather (Cotton Mather's father), preached a sermon against the trials. He agreed with his son that the Devil could take the form of any person he chose. But, Increase said, the Devil could be playing tricks on the townspeople of Salem all on his own, without involving any of the victims. Increase and Cotton Mather both urged the Court to disregard spectral evidence. After all, as Increase wrote, "better that ten suspected witches should escape than one innocent person should be condemned." On October 29, the Court of Oyer and Terminer was disbanded, and many of the people who were still rotting in jail were released.

The looming scientific revolution of the 1700s managed to whisper a bit of reason into the ears of the witch trials participants before things got too out of hand. You can't scientifically prove that someone is a witch. Nor can you scientifically prove that they're not. The important fact is this: you can't prove a negative. You can't definitively say that someone is incapable of performing witchcraft. You have to give them the benefit of the doubt.

The witch trials actually helped to banish the devil from New England. Before the trials, ministers preached that Satan walked the earth in physical form in order to tempt humankind. Afterwards, they banished the devil to Hell, and focused on the fact that he waited there to welcome sinners to the fiery depths. People started to take personal responsibility for their own sins, instead of blaming the devil for their failings.

The people themselves eventually stopped the madness before it whipped into a four-centuries-long frenzy like the Inquisition. Had they not, we'd still be hanging fractious neighbors and looking sideways at people who didn't fit society's ideas of normal. (Knowing my neighbors, I'd be the one dancing at the end of a rope.) Heck, they'd probably make a reality show out of the proceedings. And we'd be getting over the witch trials in, oh, about 2092.

But we're centuries away from the witch trials, and our culture has become comfortable with demons, even to the point that they appear in our daily lives. Since the nineteenth century, people have been seeing demons nearly every day.

SEA FOODS ★

The William Underwood Company was established in 1822. In fact, it's the oldest canning company in America. The potted meat product was originally packed in glass, and in 1836 moved to using metal tins. The company added deviled ham to their product line in 1868, and the iconic capering devil logo was trademarked in 1870, making it the oldest food trademark still in use in America. Their motto was simple and obvious: "Branded with the Devil but fit for the gods." That's by no means the only devil on the table. We serve deviled eggs at our picnics, and devil's food cake at our birthday parties.

Fiend Oil, dating back to the 1930s, lubricates and cleans firearms and chrome, and acts as a rust preventative. Matches, back in the day, were called lucifers, because of their ability to bring light with a simple sharp scrape. All of this advertising used demons as a recognizable shorthand, encouraging their customers to think of demons as powerful entities that could also act as helpers. Take Red Devil lye as an example. It's something muscular and nasty that goes into the dark unseen depths of your plumbing system to clean out gunk. Here is a feared entity whose power has been harnessed to help humanity.

While this book was being written, Dirt Devil vacuum cleaners went viral with their spoof of the movie *The Exorcist*. A woman nervously ushers a priest into her home. They cautiously make their way deeper into the house. Terrifying shrieks come from behind a closed bedroom door. When the priest opens the door, a young girl is plastered to the ceiling, her mouth twisted open in a pleading shriek for help. She is suddenly yanked back and forth on the ceiling, a victim helpless against the awesome power ... of the vacuum cleaner that the woman upstairs is happily, obliviously wielding as the camera pans up one floor.

So here's the question: at what point does the iconography of the Devil become so cartoonish that advertisers feel comfortable about putting it on product labels? When does the image of the Devil become innocuous enough that designers will use it without fear of offending Christian consumers? How far can advertisers skate to the edge?

This familiarity with demons isn't limited to advertising. It has slithered its way into other facets of popular culture too.

Every student of popular film can trace the evolution of movie monsters. In the 1920s and 1930s, we borrowed classic movie monsters from literature – Dracula, Frankenstein – and from the darkest corners of our nightmares – the Mummy, come to staggering life.

With World War II, though, we realized that there were bigger monsters on the front page of the morning newspaper than in the movie listings. In a world where a Hitler or a Stalin could murder millions of his own people, Flash Gordon fighting Ming the Merciless seemed kind of childish.

The classic movie monsters became a joke, foils for Abbott and Costello instead of getting top billing. The horror movies of the 1950s and 1960s dealt with more immediate threats than a shambling, dusty pharaoh or a stitched-together electrified corpse. *The Creature from the Black Lagoon, The Blob*, and the other flickering terrors of that era were the product of the horrors of the nuclear age.

The Devil has crept back into popular culture, along with the rest of the classic movie-monster line up – because of course they never really left us. But now, all of these monsters demand to be treated more with respect than regarded with fear. They have integrated themselves into human society. Anne Rice's rock star vampires opened the door for a more human monster. The demons of Supernatural trade banter with the Winchester brothers. The Devil kept his forked tail, and along the way, he also picked up a pitchfork, red skin, and a neatly trimmed van Dyke beard.

Entertainment dealing with the supernatural is especially popular with teens. On the cusp of adulthood, craving independence yet still living at home and chafing under parental rules, many teens seek a way to develop a sense of personal power.

Pat Gill is a professor of media studies at the University of Illinois at Urbana-Champaign. She says that supernatural slasher movies – the stomping grounds of Freddy Krueger, Jason Voorhees, and Michael Myers – are popular with teens because they can relate to the main characters in the movies, who are often teens themselves. Parents in slasher films are usually depicted as aloof and uncaring, oftentimes absent figures that leave the teenage characters to fight the monsters on their own. Gill points out that parent characters tend to be "stupid, they are selfish, they don't listen, they don't seem to care about their kids. Or if they do care, they are unable to help their kids face the nightmares of the everyday world."

Devils, of course, hopped off of the movie screen and into everyday life long ago. The Go Devil was the army's nickname for the engine in the Willys MB Jeep produced during World War II. It powered all of the Jeeps built for the United States and the Allies, and was later used in civilian Jeeps. The first two Go Devil engines powered the prototype Willys Quad, built in 1940 for the US Army to compete against the British reconnaissance car. The Willys Quad was overweight by Army standards, but the Go Devil engine had a heavier transmission. The combination turned out to work better for strenuous cross-country travel. The Willys Go Devil had a better power-to-weight ratio than any sports car available in the late 1930s – and the Army gave it to eighteen year olds to tool around Europe in.

The Northwestern State University of Louisiana sports teams, the Demons, rally behind their purple mascot Vic the Demon. (The "Vic" is short for "Victory".) The DePaul University Blue Demons have their mascot DIBS (Demon In a Blue Suit) to jump around on the sidelines. Devils are one of the most common mascots for sports teams in the United States, probably because Christianity is one of the dominant religions in America. Demon mascots can be fierce and intimidating, or mischievous and cute, with no spiritual connotations at all. Most teams with mascots such as "Devils" or "Demons" aren't meant to have any religious significance. They're simply chosen to intimidate opponents. This is the same reason sports teams are named Sharks or Bears or Timberwolves, and not Chipmunks or Fluffy Bunny Rabbits.

Because we are a predominantly Christian country, with a predominantly Christian history, that history, and our present culture, is littered with references to God and the Devil. Even if the devil references aren't intended to be diabolical, they're around nonetheless.

5. THE DEVIL WENT DOWN TO GEORGIA: THE DEMONIC IN MUSIC

"One night, in the year 1713 I dreamed I had made a pact with the devil for my soul. Everything went as I wished: my new servant anticipated my every desire. Among other things, I gave him my violin to see if he could play. How great was my astonishment on hearing a sonata so wonderful and so beautiful, played with such great art and intelligence, as I had never even conceived in my boldest flights of fantasy. I felt enraptured, transported, enchanted: my breath failed me and – I awoke.

I immediately grasped my violin in order to retain, in part at least, the impression of my dream. In vain!"

Giuseppe Tartini (1692-1770) was an Italian composer and violinist of the late Baroque-early Classical era. He composed over four hundred pieces, focusing on violin concerti and sonatas. Unusually for that era, he composed no church music or operas.

Tartini is best known for his piece "The Devil's Trill Sonata" (1713). The music for this fiendishly complicated piece came to him in a dream. Tartini dreamed he had sold his soul to the devil, and it was working out fabulously. Half-joking, he turned to his new buddy and handed Satan his violin, essentially saying "show me what you've got". The Devil started to play with such amazing virtuosity that Tartini was left breathless with admiration.

When the composer awoke, he lunged for his instrument, trying to capture the infernal music he'd heard in his dream. His audiences loved the result, but of course, Tartini knew that his composition was just a pale shadow of the brilliant music his subconscious had treated him to while he was asleep.

The insanely talented 19th century musician Niccolo Paganini was said to have sold his soul to the Devil. How else to explain his infernal mastery of the violin, considered to be Satan's favorite instrument? After all, the Devil didn't go down to Georgia to tear it up on the clarinet.

Paganini was one of the greatest violin virtuosos who ever lived. He learned to play the mandolin at the age of five, and he was composing by the time he was seven. He started performing publicly at age twelve, but by the time he was sixteen, he had suffered a breakdown and disappeared into alcoholism. He clawed his way back to sobriety, and by the age of 22 he was a superstar.

Paganini was very pale and extremely thin, with long black hair that would fall wildly into his face as he played. He was just as much a showman as any modern rock star. He was rumored to cut halfway through three of his violin strings before a performance. As he played with wild abandon, the strings would snap, one at a time, until Paganini was left performing incredible passages on the one remaining string. (This could also have been the result of Paganini's preference for thinner gut strings, in comparison to the thicker strings popular with earlier musicians. The purity of his sound was due to his use of thinner strings. Another feature of his particular style was the pizzicato, or "plucking," accompaniment with the left hand. This is also very rough on strings.)

Once, before a performance, Paganini was requested to bring a note to the concertmaster from his mother, in which she swore that the Devil was not Paganini's father.

Paganini's mother was fond of recounting a dream she'd had when the famous musician was still a child, in which an angel appeared to her. She had prayed that her young son become a great violinist, and the angel magnanimously granted her request. This angelic stamp of approval didn't do much to tarnish Paganini's demonic reputation. In 1831, he wrote to a friend complaining that in Vienna, he had been associated quite strongly with the Devil.

At a concert, Paganini had played a piece he had written called "Le Streghe" (The Witches). He had composed the piece after being inspired by a ballet by Vigano, with music by Sussmayr, called *Il Noce di Benevento*. The ballet had a snappy little tune just at the point where a coven of witches makes an appearance on the stage. Paganini composed a set of variations for violin and orchestra on this tune, which everyone in Milan seemed to be whistling or humming. After the concert, a member of the audience had given his impression of Paganini's performance.

"The individual, who was represented to me as of a sallow complexion, melancholy air, and bright eyes, affirmed that he saw nothing surprising in my performance, for he had distinctly seen … the devil at my elbow directing my arm and guiding my bow. My resemblance to him was proof of my origin. He was clothed in red – had horns on his head – and carried his tail between his legs. After so minute a description, you will understand, sir, it was impossible to doubt the fact; hence, many concluded that they had discovered the secret of what they termed my wonderful feats …" This beautifully snarky letter must have felt so good to write as the violinist vented to his friend, his pen scratching out the words.

In truth, the early 19th century in Europe was ripe for the idea of a supernaturally artistic virtuoso. It was the age of Romanticism, and exhibitionism, escapism, vulgarity, and preoccupation with the occult were merely the order of the day. The Europe in which Paganini performed had just gone through the French Revolution, followed by the Napoleonic Wars. Nerves were on edge after years of fighting. Paganini's showmanship raised him to the status of a cult hero. He seems to have enjoyed the attention – and the box office receipts. But he also seems to have rued the fact that it gave him such an unsavory reputation. Being in league with the Devil is fine for a rising young star, but Paganini seems to have regretted, at the end of his life, being typecast.

But, in the end, Paganini accepted the role of virtuoso. "I've never found it worth my while to deny publicly all the silly nonsense circulated about me. If I please people as an artist, then they can believe all the romantic tales they like."

It didn't help Paganini's post-mortem reputation that he died without receiving Last Rites. In May 1840, he was ill enough that the Bishop of Nice sent a parish priest to give the famous musician the final sacrament. Paganini refused, thinking the offer premature. (It was, but not by much.) A week later, he died from internal hemorrhaging before a priest could be called. Because of this, and his reputed deal with the Devil, the Catholic Church denied him a Christian burial. After an appeal to the Pope, his body was transported to Genoa, but he still wasn't buried. His remains were finally buried in Parma in 1876, but in 1893, his body was dug up for a viewing.

He was finally buried for good in a different cemetery in Parma in 1896, 56 years after he died.

Hildegard von Bingen, one of Western music's earliest known composers, wrote a morality play in 1151 called Ordo Virtutum. The role of the Devil demanded a special singing technique called *strepitus diaboli,* meaning "singing in a low, growling voice".

The violin isn't the only instrument that has been demonized. In 1841, Adolphe Sax, the son of Belgium's chief instrument maker, submitted to the national exhibition his latest invention. It was a hybrid of brass and reed that joined a clarinet mouthpiece and the keywork of a flute to the body of an ophicleide, a sinuous horn with a conical flared bell. The instrument had an undeniably sexy sound – its timbres mimicked the human voice. It would later become known, in a nod to its creator, as the saxophone.

In a letter to his brother written shortly before he died, Adolphe Sax wrote of a dream he'd had in which black devils were playing his horn and summoning all the damned to the fiery pits of Hell.

In the 20th century, the saxophone became the most prominent instrument in jazz, the devil's music. The saxophone's carnal nature and association with dance music horrified the higher-ups in the church. In 1903, Pope Pius X wrote a treatise which prohibited the use of certain instruments "that may give reasonable cause for disgust or scandal". He wrote that the saxophone was "unworthy of the House of Prayer and of the Majesty of God" and banned its use in church music.

On April 20, 1832, Paganini gave a charity concert for the victims of a cholera epidemic in Paris, which would have an effect on another musician. Franz Liszt attended the concert, and was entranced. Paganini's playing spurred him to become as great a virtuoso on the piano as Paganini was on the violin.

As a composer, Liszt made good use of a bizarre, discordant series of musical notes called the tritone, or "devil's interval". Early composers tended to avoid using this extremely dissonant chord just because it sounded unpleasant in the context of Baroque music. There's no evidence that the Church ever banned or punished its use; composers of the era just chose not to use it for aesthetic reasons. The tritone didn't even get its demonic nickname until much later, in the Romantic Era – the time of Niccolo Paganini and Franz Liszt. Liszt became so popular that he evolved into a proto-rockstar in spite of his use of the unpleasantly dissonant tritone in his composing.

The tritone's influence reached far beyond classical music. Black Sabbath's guitar player, Tony Iommi, jumped on the devil's interval in his composing. It was just a happy accident for Iommi that the chord sounded so weird and ominous. In an interview for BBC News Magazine in 2006, he said that it was never his intention to shroud the band in an aura of evil. He said, "When I started writing Sabbath stuff it was just something that sounded right. I didn't think I was going to make it Devil music."

There's a fascinating back-and-forth going on here. Black Sabbath has the reputation of being a fearsomely Satanic heavy metal band. Their music is loud and dark and dissonant. But if you look at the lyrics, almost every reference to the Devil or to evil also contains a warning against dabbling in black magic. Black Sabbath's sound may be terrifying, but their lyrics are more the warnings of a biblical prophet than a glorification of evil for evil's sake. Michael Moynihan, author of *Lords of Chaos*, writes that the band's lyrics "reveal an almost Christian fear of demons and sorcery." That's an interesting take on a band with such an ominous reputation.

Ozzy Osbourne, the lead singer of Black Sabbath, has faced his share of controversy. His music has been linked to several suicide pacts, one involving three teenage boys. One of the boys shot himself while listening to the song "Suicide Solution." The boy (and others too) interpreted the lyrics as "I tell you to end your life." Actually, that's just Ozzy's famously mush-mouthed singing gumming up the works. The line is really "I tell you to *enjoy* life/ I wish I could but it's too late."

In 1993, three eight-year-old boys were killed and mutilated, and their bodies dumped near a muddy drainage ditch in West Memphis, Arkansas. Three teenagers were quickly arrested for the gruesome crime. They'd been marked as troublemakers already, and had previously been arrested for vandalism and other petty crimes. But the nail in the coffin for Damien Echols, Jason Baldwin, and Jesse Misskelly Jr. was their love of heavy metal music.

The West Memphis Three, as the defendants became known, were fans of Metallica, and on this fact is what the prosecution based much of its case. The teenagers were labeled as Satanists because of their taste in music. The prosecution pointed out that Echols, seen as the demonic ringleader, had an interest in pagan religion as well as in heavy metal. This combination was the kiss of death in the Bible Belt. Echols was a fan of Metallica, and copied lyrics from their songs into his journal. He was convicted in 1994 for the murder of the three young boys, and spent eighteen years on death row for murders he didn't commit. He was released in August 2011.

The public outcry and hysteria surrounding the trial of the West Memphis Three was not just a case of brooding teenagers, who dressed in black and listened to heavy metal, being pegged as delinquents (and later, murderers). Their prosecution was the most dramatic incident of a growing fear of the infernal influence of rock music, particularly heavy metal.

Elyse Marie Pahler was fifteen years old on July 22, 1995 when she snuck out of her California home to meet three teenage boys at Nipoma Mesa. The boys murdered her there, in a bid to get their heavy metal band Hatred "the madness to go pro."

Elyse's parents, David and Lisanne Pahler, attempted to sue the band Slayer, saying that the band's music seduced the boys into murdering their daughter. All three boys were Slayer fans, and actually admitted that the lyrics of the songs influenced them. Joseph Fiorella, who was sixteen at the time of the murder, told a counselor a year later, "It gets inside your head. It's almost embarrassing that I was so influenced by the music." But Jacob Delashmutt put a different spin on things in an interview for the *Washington Post*. "The music is destructive but that's not why Elyse was murdered. She was murdered because Joe was obsessed with her, and obsessed with killing her."

David Pahler insisted the case was not about art, or about First Amendment rights, but about marketing. The case was eventually dismissed. Judge E. Jeffrey Burke upheld Slayer's right to free speech. "There's not a legal position that could be taken that would make Slayer responsible for the girl's death. Where do you draw the line? You might as well start looking through the library at every book on the shelf."

In 2001, Paul Bostaph, Slayer's drummer, made his opinion known. "They're trying to blame the whole thing on us. That's such nonsense. If you're gonna do something stupid like that, you should get in trouble for it." (He also noted that the murderers hadn't even followed the instructions for the rituals correctly.)

The song "Sympathy for the Devil" by the Rolling Stones is a song of great power. It was recorded by the Stones in June 1968 for their *Beggar's Banquet* album. It's got a good samba beat, with an upbeat rhythm of conga drums, and maracas shaking a lively accompaniment. It's a song you can groove to. Mick Jagger said the song was good dance music. "It doesn't speed up or slow down. It keeps this constant [rhythm]. It becomes less pretentious because it is a very unpretentious groove."

The lyrics are strong and self-assured. The song references many of the atrocities throughout history, beginning with the crucifixion of Jesus and continuing through the religious wars of Europe, the Russian Revolution and the massacre of the Imperial family, and World War Two. "Sympathy for the Devil" came out of the late 1960s, the era of Woodstock and Altamont. It was a time of high emotions, when loyalties were strictly divided. The Vietnam War, civil rights, rights for women – these were all highly divisive issues. People, especially young people who were listening to rock music, were primed to feel these issues deep in their hearts. People fought for what they believed in. At Kent State, they even died for it. Somehow, the music of Weezer or Lady Gaga just doesn't have the same effect.

In the episode of the Muppet Show where Alice Cooper is the guest host, Alice tries to sell the Muppets a contract that promises fabulous riches and worldwide fame in return for their souls. Most of the Muppets steer clear of the offer, but Gonzo actively pursues the deal. In the end, he can't find a pen to sign away his soul, and he rushes around the backstage area in a fit of frustration. "Does anybody have a pen? I'd sell my SOUL for a pen! …. Wait, I got other plans for that…"

The rocker Jerry Lee Lewis was raised in the Assemblies of God Church, although unlike most Pentecostals, he did not repent of his sins, trust in Jesus for his salvation, and dedicate his life to the Lord. He did enroll at the Southwestern Bible Institute in Waxahachie, Texas, and even preached a little, but was thrown out of school for playing a boogie-woogie version of the hymn "My God Is Real" for one morning assembly. Jerry Lee's signature piano style developed from a mixture of jazzed up Pentecostal hymns, hillbilly boogie, and black rhythm and blues.

Jerry Lee had always been conflicted about religion. His mother was very religious, and Jerry Lee went so far as to do a little preaching at the bible college. But the rhythm of rock and roll had a strong pull. There's a famous recording that was made at the Sun Records studio in Memphis in 1957, when Jerry Lee was about to record "Great Balls of Fire." He and the owner of Sun Records, Sam Phillips, were deep into a discussion of whether or not rock and roll was "wholesome." Someone started the recording early, and the conversation was caught on tape.

Jerry Lee was outspoken in his opinion that rock and roll was "the devil's music," and the song he was about to record was no exception. Phillips argued that rock and roll was made to make people feel good, and anything that made people feel good couldn't possibly be evil. It could, in fact, lead to salvation. Jerry Lee snapped, "How can the Devil save souls? What are you talkin' about? I have the Devil in me. If I didn't, I'd be a Christian."

Jerry Lee Lewis had a cousin, Jimmy, who would come with him to sneak into the juke joints to hear the bands play. At first, Jimmy was excited about it, but when the two boys were actually standing underneath the bar windows, Jimmy chickened out and ran home, leaving Jerry Lee to enjoy the hoppin' blues by himself. It's not surprising Jimmy suffered from a guilty conscience when it came to sneaking into the forbidden bars – he grew up to become the famed preacher Jimmy Swaggart.

Elvis Presley was another one of those early rock and roll stars who drew criticism from the church. In fact, much of Elvis' early life was a battle between the secular and the divine. His great-uncle, Gains Mansell, helped build the small wooden church where Elvis was taught the infallibility of the Bible. Elvis sat through the services, but was terrified by the hellfire and brimstone preaching. He believed in God, but he couldn't reconcile that faith with the preachers trying to make people feel guilty for things they hadn't done.

Elvis' mother, Gladys, was very spiritual, and shared that deep faith with her son. But Elvis' father, Vernon, was not a religious man. When he took Elvis to see his first movie, "Abbott and Costello Meet Frankenstein," it had to be their secret, kept from Gladys to escape her wrath. The church frowned on frivolities like motion pictures. It's ironic that the movies turned out to be one of Elvis' paths to fame and fortune.

The delicious dichotomy of Elvis' story doesn't end there. American Pentecostalism, which was the most vocal critic of early rock and roll, saw any kind of aberrant sexuality – premarital sex, the gyrating hips of "Elvis the Pelvis" – as an invitation to wallow in demonic influence.

However, the Pentecostals do encourage their congregants to give themselves over to the divine ecstasy of dance, music, and speaking in tongues. (This behavior is seen by more mainstream sects of Christianity as veering dangerously close to devil worship all by itself.)

The beautifully ironic thing about all this is that Elvis, like Jerry Lee Lewis, was also raised in the Assemblies of God Church – which is an offshoot of Pentecostalism. He admitted these contradictions in several interviews. Elvis gained his deep appreciation of gospel music from Sundays spent in a church pew, his soul drinking in the music of worship. He recalled a youth spent in the energy of the church, being swept up by hellfire and brimstone preaching and the ecstasy of worship. "They said I was 'controversial' … Hell, all I did was what came naturally, what I learned when I was a little kid in church, movin' my body to the music."

By the 1970s, rock had become theatrical. Rock concerts were elaborate productions, with stage sets that rivaled Broadway shows. Alice Cooper, the Rolling Stones, and Black Sabbath drew crowds of screaming fans. KISS showed up soon after that, in full makeup, spitting blood and blowing fire on stage. Gene Simmons once said, "We wanted to look like we crawled out from under a rock in Hell. We wanted parents to look at us and instantly want to throw up." Imitation being the sincerest form of flattery, KISS fans started to show up at concerts in makeup just like the band. KISS became so famous that rumors inevitably began to swirl about the true meaning of their band name. Some said it stood for "Knights in Satan's Service." Paul Stanley snarked back that it actually meant "Kids in Sunday School."

The band AC/DC also came under fire. Their first big hit was "Highway to Hell," and didn't *that* get people wondering. But Angus Young, the guitarist, soon set the record straight in an interview with the *Los Angeles Times*. "It has nothing to do with devil worship. We toured four years at a stretch with no break. A guy asked how would you best describe our tours. We said 'a highway to hell.' All we'd done is describe what it is like to be on the road for four years. When you're sleeping with the singer's socks two inches from your nose, believe me, that's pretty close to hell." In another interview, Young made his position even more clear. "We're not black magic Satanists. I don't drink blood. I may wear black underpants now and again, but that's it."

Even bands that don't actually exist use the symbolism of the demonic in their stage presence. The fictional band Spinal Tap used a fearsome horned skull as the backdrop to one of their shows. By the time the mockumentary *This Is Spinal Tap* came out in 1984, demonic imagery had become a trope for many heavy metal bands.

Led Zeppelin rose to fame very quickly amid rumors of dark bargains. Robert Plant and Jimmy Page were devoted fans of Robert Johnson's music, even going so far as to borrow lyrics from the blues icon. It's been suggested that Robert Plant even had a special mojo amulet – a glass vial filled with dirt from the very crossroads where Johnson sold his soul to the Devil.

Led Zeppelin was rumored to have made their own pact with the Devil – fame and fortune in exchange for their immortal souls. Three of the four band members supposedly signed the infernal contract in early 1968, but one of the musicians refused. Even now, if you ask someone familiar with rock music to name the four members of Led Zeppelin, the answer you're likely to get is "Oh, that's easy. Robert Plant, Jimmy Page, John Bonham … and … and … and the other guy." John Paul Jones was said to be the only band member who refused to sign up with Satan. Oddly enough, he was also the only band member who remained untouched by the bad luck that dogged Page, Plant, and Bonham, bad luck that included vicious hauntings, terrible accidents, even death.

The lyrics to the most famous Led Zeppelin song of all, "Stairway to Heaven," seem to reference the occult. Robert Plant sings "there are two paths you can go by" and "there's still time to change the road you're on". "Two paths" can easily be interpreted as the left-hand and right-hand paths, one evil, one good, one leading to Hell, the other to Heaven.

"Stairway to Heaven" is also one of many rock songs that is said to contain either backward masks or phonetic reversals. (A backward mask is a message that shows up when a recording is played backward. A phonetic reversal is a recording made and then turned over, with lyrics written using the same basic sounds)

Starting with the verse that begins with "If there's a bustle in your hedgerow…" and continuing until "and it makes me wonder," there is a phonetic reversal that is said to be a prayer to Satan. If you play that section backward, you may be able to decipher phrases that sound like "here's to my sweet Satan. The one will be the sad one who makes me sad and whose power is in Satan." The next line is said to be either "He'll be with you, Satan Satan Satan," or "He will give you 666". The last line seems to say "So follow him in worship, bring me yourself, my sad Satan." (This "poetry" all seems a bit woolly)

The last phrase, the delicate, evocative "And she's buying a stairway to Heaven" is also said to contain a backward phrase. Some listeners claim to hear "Play music backward, hear words sung."

Led Zeppelin was not alone in this circus. Electric Light Orchestra was one of the first bands that was accused of placing hidden satanic messages in their songs. The early ELO song "Eldorado" supposedly had a phonetic reversal sequence that said, "He is the nasty one. Christ you're infernal. It is said we're dead men. All who have the mark will live."

Jeff Lynne, the leader of ELO, stated in a radio interview that the claim was "a load of rubbish." His defense made perfect sense. "Anybody who can write a song forward and have it say something else backward, has got to be some kind of genius and that I ain't."

Even the Christian rock band Petra got into the act. On their *More Power To You* album, there is a backward track just before the song "Judas Kiss." When the track is reversed, a voice asks, "What are you looking for the Devil for? When you ought to be looking for the Lord?"

And a backward track on the B-52s song "Detour Through Your Mind," from the 1986 album *Bouncing Off the Satellites,* cattily points out, "Oh no, you're playing the record backwards. Watch out, you might ruin your needle."

6. SATANISM AND THE "SATANIC PANIC"

I grew up in the 1970s and 1980s, in a religious family. I was raised in a Russian branch of the Orthodox Christian church. During my grade school years, my parents were exceedingly concerned about sects. I remember serious discussions around the dinner table, lectures that contained incessant warnings about the Hare Krishnas, the Moonies, and any other group that seemed remotely suspect. (Although where my sister and I would have encountered Hare Krishnas in the Chicago suburbs kind of escapes me now.) My parents drilled these warnings into our heads even more than telling us about "stranger danger."

My husband had it even worse. His family was not particularly religious, but he still got in serious trouble just for having a couple of geodes and a copy of a Time-Life supernatural series book in his room. We both grew up in the thick of the Satanic Panic. I can clearly remember staring at the Proctor & Gamble logo on the back of some shampoo bottle in our upstairs bathroom, trying to parse the symbolism I had been assured was there, trying to see what was so offensive about it. I remember my mom and my aunt discussing it in hushed tones, and the nuns at the Catholic school going closed-mouthed and tight-lipped every time we curious students asked about it. The Satanic Panic was a fairly large part of my childhood.

Then I grew up and discovered that none of it really happened.

People have tried for centuries to figure out where, exactly, Satan came from. The general Christian party line is that Lucifer was one of God's favored angels, the Light Bearer, the one who sat at God's right hand. In this version, long before Man was created, Lucifer rebelled against God and was cast out of Heaven, along with his followers. A third of the angelic host chose to follow Lucifer out of Heaven, and became Satan's army of demons. Because of the exalted angelic nature of demons, once they renounced God, they could never go back on that decision. (We humans, though, can be forgiven for our sins time after time, as long as we repent and are truly sorry for those sins. That's what gives us the advantage over demons.)

But that story, as all good stories do, became embellished over the years with retelling. If we take it as read that the God vs. Satan story includes several key points – Satan and his demons hate God and anything divine, mankind is an expendable pawn in the spiritual battle between good and evil, and Satan will ultimately be banished to the realm of Hell, away from God for eternity – we can see that Satanism has existed in different forms since well before Christianity.

Many pre-Christian religions have at their heart a conflict between the forces of good and the forces of evil. The Canaanites performed child sacrifices to Baal, and the Jews adopted Baal as another name for Satan. The Zoroastrian religion of ancient Persia had the great conflict between Ahuramazda, the god of light, and Ahriman, the god of darkness. The Egyptians had their light and dark opposites as well. Osiris, the good god, was even temporarily vanquished by the evil god Set. Set, Osiris' brother, invited all the gods to a banquet. An ornate, richly decorated casket was displayed in a place of honor at the banquet. Set offered the casket to anyone who could fit inside it. The gods all tried – and when Osiris climbed inside, Set slammed the lid on him and tossed the casket into the Nile, drowning his brother. Then Set cut Osiris' body into pieces and scattered it across the length of Egypt. Osiris' wife, Isis, retrieved the pieces and revived Osiris, who became the benevolent lord of death and the underworld.

So there was a rich tradition of light versus dark even before Christianity came onto the scene. In the early days of the church, when the Christian philosophy was still getting sorted out, some sects of Christianity spent a lot of intellectual effort refining the idea of who, exactly, Satan was. The dualist heresies of the Middle Ages were especially invested in this idea.

For example, the Bulgarian Bogomile sect, which originated in Macedonia in the tenth century, and really took hold in Russia a couple of centuries later, taught that Satan and Jesus were brothers, Satan being the elder. The antagonism between the two didn't really start until Jesus was chosen to save mankind, leaving Satan as the bad guy. (There's a whole lot of very human conflict going on in this particular heresy. We see our religions through the lens of our own human experience. We can't help it.)

The Bogomils taught that God had two sons, Satanail, the elder, and Michael, the younger. The elder son rebelled against God, and became evil. After his fall from Heaven, he created the world and tried to create mankind, but he had to appeal to God to breathe the spirit of life into his creation. Adam was allowed to till the ground on the condition that he sell himself and his descendants to the owner of said ground – Satanail. Much later, Michael was sent down to earth in human form, becoming Jesus. He was baptized by John, and selected by God to save humanity from Adam's bargain with Satanail. The Holy Spirit – Michael, again – hovered over Jesus' head in the form of a dove. With this grace, Jesus became Michael, the vanquisher of Satan, in human form. Jesus received the power to break the clay tablet that represented the covenant between Adam and Satanail. He conquered Satanail, and took away his god powers, removing the divine suffix –il from his name. Thus, Satanail the god became Satan the deposed spirit.

The Bogomils believed that God created man's soul, but Satan created all matter – including the dust that later became Man. This is derived from an earlier mid-seventh century heresy, Paulicianism, which taught that there were two gods: a good God who had created men's souls, and an evil God who had created the physical universe including the human body.

Manichaeism is another early heresy, and another dualist sect, meaning the basis of the sect is a belief in a struggle between good and evil. Manichaeism, Zoroastrianism, and Christianity were all vying for social and political influence in the first centuries of the Common Era, and for a while, Christianity had some pretty stiff competition from Zoroastrianism and Manichaeism. They were all dualist religions, all with a convincing story to tell about the nature of good and evil. Manichaeism was even very tolerant of other religions such as Buddhism, incorporating Buddhist teachings like transmigration of souls.

The great Christian Saint Augustine (354–430) started out as a Manichaean. Some scholars feel that the Manichaean philosophy influenced some of Augustine's ideas, such as his concept of Hell, the nature of good and evil, and his hostility to earthly pleasures of the flesh and to sexual activity. Augustine, however, converted to Christianity in 387. Augustine, it seems, converted for two very good reasons. One, he came to realize that the Manichaean belief that knowledge was the key to salvation was too passive, and didn't result in real, lasting change in one's spiritual life.

The other reason was simple survival. The Roman Emperor Theodosius I issued a decree of death for all Manichaeans in 382. In 391, he declared Christianity to be the only legitimate religion for the Roman Empire. At its height, Manichaeism was one of the most widespread religions in the world, and was briefly the main rival to Christianity in the jostle to replace classical paganism. But Christianity muscled its way to the top, decrying the many other dualist sects as heresy.

These off-branches of Christianity continued, through the Manichaeans to the Bogomils to the Cathars, with the Inquisitors of the thirteenth century stomping on all of them.

Modern English has inherited a word from all of this heresy-stomping. The word "buggery" emerged, by way of the French "bougre," from the Latin "Bugarus," meaning

Bulgarian. "Buggery" first appeared in English in 1330, but its original meaning was "abominable heresy." It didn't take on a sexual connotation until 1555.

The Cathars were perhaps the first sect to actively encourage the worship of Satan. The Cathars saw God and Satan as equal, if opposite. Cathar dogma saw both of these spirits as gods, a god of love and a god of power. Since it obviously took quite a bit of power to create the world, and since love is incompatible with supreme power, the God of love could not have created the world. That task fell to another god, a god of evil, the god of the world – Rex Mundi, as the Cathars knew him. Material creation is a manifestation of power, therefore (to the Cathars) material creation – the world in which we live – is inherently evil.

The Cathars followed the beliefs of the Gnostics (from the Greek word "gnosis," or knowledge). The Gnostics believed that God was good, but the created world – Satan's dominion – was evil. Gnostic philosophy continued throughout the Middle Ages as a way to explain the rampant evil in the world.

Interestingly, all these heresies throughout the Middle Ages provided ample fodder for modern Satanists as a cornucopia of origin stories. It all boils down, really, to an imagined conversation between God and Satan:

Satan: So let me get this straight. You made us, the angels, perfect in every way.
God: Yup.
Satan: And you made Man out of mud, you made him imperfect, and you gave him free will, so if he wants to ignore you instead of worshipping you, he can do that, with no repercussions whatsoever.
God: (nodding) Uh-huh.
Satan: And you decided that Man was your favored creature, and that angels should watch over him, protect him, and serve him, even though he's done nothing to deserve such preferential treatment.
God: Got it in one.
Satan: Screw this. I'm outta here.

The heretics – the Manichaeans, then the Bogomils, then the Cathars, along with plenty of others – seem to be the only sects of Christianity with the imagination to envision this conversation. Later, it was the Satanists who imagined it. We can, if we want, look at Satanism as a heretical sect of Christianity, one that pragmatically calls a spade a spade.

There is, however, one big problem with this. Traditional Satanists seem to be content with keeping to themselves. A Satanist certainly doesn't worship God – but he doesn't worship Satan, either. A traditional Satanist is an atheist at heart, choosing to follow his own physical desires rather than worship *any* god. Religious Satanists tend to be ... well, snobs. They see demons as symbols of different parts of the human ego. Satan represents the entire ego. To a Satanist, the Dark Lord and his minions are nothing more than philosophical constructs. They aren't objects of worship or devotion. The only creature a Satanist is devoted to is himself.

The 1970s saw a huge surge in Devil-themed entertainment. This was the decade of the infernal in Hollywood, seeing the release of such cult classics as *Dark Shadows, The Omen, Children Shouldn't Play With Dead Things, The Amityville Horror, The Exorcism of Emily Rose*, and the granddaddy of all demonic movies, *The Exorcist*. This hyper-awareness of the Devil in the 1970s led quite naturally, in the 1980s, to the Satanic Panic.

The Satanic Panic really got going in 1980, with the publication of *Michelle Remembers*, a book of dubious provenance that was supposedly a transcript of the conversations between a woman named Michelle Smith and her psychotherapist. It's a sensationally detailed book about the abuses Smith suffered at the hands of a satanic cult her mother belonged to. It's generally been debunked, along with much of the rest of the "satanic panic." (And it wasn't terribly hard to debunk, either. For instance, the Church of Satan was described as being older than the Christian Church. In actuality, the Church of Satan was founded by Anton LaVey in 1966.)

To make things even more awkward for misfit teenagers everywhere, the early 1980s also saw the publication of the first edition of the *Dungeons and Dragons* play manual, *Deities and Demigods*. The role-playing game had immediately developed a bad reputation outside the wood-paneled basements in which it was played, and the *Deities and Demigods* manual didn't help matters. The *Monster Manual* was even more suspect, listing twelve demons and eleven types of devils one could encounter playing the game in the D&D universe. (The company that published the game and its accompanying manuals, TSR, was so concerned about the public outcry that the words "demon" and "devil" were removed from the second edition of the rules. They were replaced with the words "tana'ri" and "baatezu", exotic enough for fantasy game play but carefully calculated to soothe critics.)

It was in the mid-1980s that things really got out of hand. The Proctor & Gamble situation is the classic example of how rumor and hearsay can blow perfectly ordinary things out of proportion. The effects of the rumor mill can be felt for years. Proctor & Gamble is a multi-million dollar company that mostly makes pet foods, cleaning agents, and personal care products. In 1980, its logo was a quaintly old-fashioned crescent moon face looking at thirteen stars, representing the thirteen original states. The rumor began circulating that if you connected the stars, lurking in the logo would be the satanic symbol "666." The rumor further theorized that the "owner" of Proctor & Gamble (whoever that might be) had made a contract with the Devil, promising a tithe of the company's massive profits to the Church of Satan.

Letters started pouring into the company's headquarters – angry, curious, hateful, abusive. By 1982 the flood had grown to five hundred letters a day. The company had to hire four staff members just to deal with the rising tide of letters.

More worrisome was the brazen vandalism of company vehicles right in the parking lot, and the boycotts against Proctor & Gamble products.

The company fought back. It sent out letters from leading fundamentalist and Catholic clergy, refuting the allegations. They eventually sent these letters out to forty-eight thousand churches. What's more, the company brought lawsuits against anyone they could identify as actively promoting the rumors. Even with all this damage control, the rumors persisted. When they died down in one area of the country, they flared up in another area, moving from the Bible Belt in the South to the fundamentalist Midwest.

In April 1985, Proctor & Gamble announced that it would remove the offending logo from all of its products. But the taint of the occult was too strong. Word of mouth is a powerful thing, and the company's lawsuits against individuals were no match for the communication network of church newsletters and flyers handed out in shopping centers. A Satanic conspiracy rumor is a juicy thing, with amazing longevity. Urban legends have legs.

At least 62 rumor-panics have occurred in rural areas of the United States alone since 1984. Rural areas of the country are more likely to experience shared social stress, like a high unemployment rate or slow economic growth. It's also in rural and small-town environments that the satanic cult scare is taken most seriously.

In a rumor-panic, there's usually one incident that starts the ball rolling – say, a Halloween party in an abandoned barn. Kids come to the party to drink and dance, maybe smoke some pot. The party usually involves loud music, too. Maybe things get a little out of hand; instruments get smashed, a car door suffers a mysterious dent that can't be explained to a suspicious parent. And then, of course, there are the kids whose parents didn't let them go to the party. They can always be counted on to spread crazy stories, and they make unimpeachable witnesses, since they weren't actually there. The stories grow, and soon, the Halloween party has turned into a satanic orgy, the punch table has become an altar with a naked woman sprawled on it, and the bonfire outside has the bones of sacrificial victims hidden in its cold ashes, just waiting for someone to come along in November to stir them to the surface.

But no one ever calls these episodes "truth-panics." It's all rumor and speculation, most of it by people who weren't even there. People love a good chewy story, especially around Halloween. (Many rumor-panics are just as seasonal as falling leaves and pumpkin spice lattes.) And stories don't get much juicier than tales of satanic ritual abuse.

Satanic ritual abuse refers to sexual abuse in the context of a satanic ritual. It actually has its roots in 17th-century Sweden, where a witch panic involved the creation of false memories and false accusations of satanic child abuse. Sweden was plagued with witch hunts in an epidemic that lasted from 1668 to 1676. The worst of these was at Torsåker, a village in central Sweden. In 1675, 71 people (6 men and 65 women, roughly a fifth of all women in the region) were beheaded and burned in a single day, one of the largest single mass killings of accused witches in recorded history.

Laurentius Hornæus, the minister of Ytterlännäs parish, was directed by Johannes Wattrangius of Torsåker parish, to investigate the accusations of witchcraft, by order of the special commission which had been created in 1674 to deal with the sudden eruption of witch hysteria. Hornæus had two boys stand at the door of the church to identify the witches as they went in by the invisible mark on their forehead. At one point, one of the boys pointed at Britta Rufina, the wife of the priest himself. After a sound slap, he quickly apologized, claiming to have been blinded by the sun.

The chief accusation against many of the witches was that they had abducted children and taken them to a witches' Sabbat at Blakulla, a famous meadow in folklore where Satan was said to hold his Sabbats. Therefore, most of the witnesses in the case were children. Hornæus's techniques were reprehensible, even by the standards of the day. Hornæus (who already had something of a terrifying reputation) extracted the required testimony from them by whippings, by dunking the children in the ice-cold water of a frozen lake, and by putting them in an oven and threatening to light the fire and bake them. Some of the witnesses suffered ill health ever afterwards and would not go anywhere near the priest's house even when grown up.

The lessons of medieval history seem to suggest that elaborate claims of satanic ritual abuse are constructed from a demonology that reaches back centuries. Most of the themes of modern abuse claims have their roots in medieval times, including secret conspiracies of Devil worshippers, midnight meetings, sexual orgies, murder of children, and cannibalism of infants in occult rituals. They are old, old stories, that reveal more about the tellers than they do about the stories' subjects.

MEDLINE is the online form of MEDLARS (the Medical Literature Analysis and Retrieval System), a database of scholarly journals held by the National Library of Medicine. This online database covers nearly fifty years of journals. But typing "satanic ritual abuse" into a MEDLINE search gives you papers going back only as far as 1991.

Most therapists agree that satanic ritual abuse involves false memories – and possibly memories implanted or implied by the therapists themselves. Some psychotherapists diagnose patients as having MPD, multiple personality disorder, and automatically make the assumption that those patients were victims of satanic ritual abuse in childhood. Here's something to think about, though: a national survey of clinical psychologists found that 1,908 psychologists reported treating no cases of ritual abuse at all during the course of their careers, and 785 reported treating only one or two cases. However, sixteen therapists reported treating having treated over a hundred cases of ritual abuse *each*. This means that some therapists are highly predisposed to see disturbed people as suffering from the effects of satanic ritual abuse, even when that may not be the case.

The interesting, and damning, feature of accusations of satanic ritual abuse is the victims' inability to produce any physical evidence that the abuse ever happened. Most, if not all, of these patients report bonfires, druggings, animal mutilations, witnessing and being forced to participate in human sacrifices of both adults and infants. It's gruesome, lurid stuff that gets passed around with the salivating eagerness of a reality television audience. Some victims "remember" attending as many as 850 rituals and watching the sacrifice of no less than twenty-five babies. In the McMartin Preschool case, animals said to have been sacrificed included a goat, a lion, and an elephant.

But when police investigate the properties where these atrocities are alleged to have taken place, there are no mass graves, no animal bones, no missing children – not so much as a cold, ashy campfire. The mutilated animals turn out to be roadkill tossed into the forest by highway workers. And the victims themselves, despite the allegations of having been tortured and cut, bear no wounds nor even scars on their bodies. The forensic evidence simply isn't there. And as the CSI fans among us know, the evidence – or the total lack of it – doesn't lie.

The Satanic Panic has been compared to both the Salem Witch Trials and the McCarthy Red Scare. This is an understandable comparison, but it's not entirely accurate.

The witch trials were a response to the accusation of the practice of witchcraft. Many of the accused were women who did practice sympathetic magic – along with most of the population. Magic was still part of the fabric of daily life at that time.

The Red Scare was a panicky overreaction to the very real threat of the Cold War. The Russians had been our allies in World War II. Then Fat Man and Little Boy, America's first atomic bombs, introduced the world to the Atomic Age, and the US-Soviet arms race was on. Spies were arrested in the United States who were leaking atomic secrets to the Russians. Joseph McCarthy saw Communists everywhere because there *were* communists around, and they had the potential to cause real harm to the United States.

The Satanic Panic, in contrast, was almost exactly the opposite. Instead of being a reaction to a problem, the threat was only *assumed* to be real. It was only after allegations had been made that anyone thought to go looking for hard physical evidence.

For a look at the zeal with which investigators hurled themselves into the project, it is worth quoting from Malcolm McGrath's *Demons in the Modern World.* During the McMartin Preschool trial, which involved particularly heinous accusations of

Satanic abuse against the owners of a California pre-school, the defense attorneys outlined the determined scope of the investigation.

The district attorneys and their assistants investigated 695 families regarding the five preschools involved. "They searched twenty-one residences, seven businesses, thirty-seven cars, three motorcycles, and one farm. They searched for child pornography, nude pictures, records, diaries, evidence of mutilated animals, bank account records, or anything else that might have been related to satanic cult activities. In the process of the investigation, 450 children and 150 adults were interviewed, forty-nine photo lineups were prepared, and bank account records were seized and examined ... Eighty-two locations were photographed and one church was investigated. In addition, three churches, two food markets, two car washes, two airports, and one national park were implicated ... Over $1 million was spent on the investigation. All these investigations uncovered not a single shred of evidence."

Satan-hunters claim that satanic cults are so secretive that they cannot be found, no matter how hard you look. They just go to ground and disappear at the slightest whiff of official trouble. But you gotta think – special agents have been infiltrating groups like the Mafia, hard-core biker gangs, drug rings, and the Ku Klux Klan for years. The police can't infiltrate secret criminal satanic covens, though. Because they don't exist.

So why did the Satanic Panic blow up like it did? There's an intriguing set of circumstances that all came together at the end of the 1970s that led to the bizarre allegations of the Satanic Panic.

During the 1970s, there was a social movement towards a greater consciousness of the rights of both women and children. For women, this was the era of Women's Lib. For children, it was the time of the child-protection movement. This new sense of responsibility was all well and good, but in the context of Satanism and the repressed-memory scare, it backfired horribly. In the case of the children, careful legal and scientific procedure fell by the wayside in the face of sensationalism. It became more important to believe the stories told by the alleged victims, than to see if those stories were actually true.

As for the spiritual side of things, there was a sudden upswing in charismatic deliverance ministries during the 1970s. Interest in exorcisms seems to follow a pattern, especially in the Catholic Church. The witch hunts of the fifteenth century began around the time of great division in the church, when there were actually two popes for a while, one in Rome and one in Avignon. In the 1970s, the church had recently undergone the upheaval of Vatican II. The time was ripe for the charismatic movement.

The Catholic charismatic movement refers to a ministry that focuses on the gifts of the Holy Spirit, including faith healing, speaking in tongues, and discernment of spirits. It was seen as a return to the ecstatic faith of the very early Church, when the apostles had received the gifts of the Spirit at Pentecost. Worship in the charismatic movement can include raising hands in prayer, praying personal prayers aloud during mass, and speaking in tongues. Deliverance ministries sprang up too, again taking the example of the early Christians.

This was also a time when ritualistic cults abounded in American society. This was the decade of the Moonies, the Hare Krishnas, and the ill-fated group that followed Jim Jones to Guyana. But even with the public alarm about these cults, very few of them had anything to do with Satanism. Furthermore, members of the actual Church of Satan would not have committed the atrocities laid at their doorstep during the Panic.

Satanism, as outlined by Anton LaVey in his books *The Satanic Bible* and *The Satanic Rituals*, is more of a hedonistic New-Age way of life than a call to the blackest evil. While Satanism does encourage sexual expression, it does so only as long as it doesn't harm anyone else. And the *Satanic Bible* specifically states: "Satanism *does not* advocate rape, child molesting, sexual defilement of animals, or any other form of sexual activity which entails the participation of those who are unwilling or whose innocence or naiveté would allow them to be intimidated or misguided into doing something against their wishes." In true Satanism, there is no organized child molesting, or cannibalism, or animal sacrifice.

Another one of the really confounding aspects of the Satanism scare, if you step back and look at it logically, is the way that the advocates of the scare place things on a sliding scale of evil. They say that participants could start out by playing Dungeons and Dragons or listening to heavy metal music, then graduate to reading the Satanic Bible. From there, it's only a matter of time before they are performing black masses and sacrificing babies.

This makes no logical sense. How can playing fantasy games turn someone into a psychopathic murderer? Psychopaths are notorious for being loners, incapable of forming any emotional attachments. Most kids who play role-playing games do it for the sense of camaraderie. What's better than getting together on a Saturday night with a bunch of other dorks, swigging Mountain Dew and turning your fingertips orange with Cheetos dust, and losing yourself in a world where you can be a high-ranking warrior-Druid-mage who kicks Orc ass – a hero?

If we take an honest look at the Church of Satan, we find a New Age message of empowerment in order to feel good. It draws people who don't fit in anywhere else, people seeking to belong. Psychopaths, brooders who don't *want* to fit in, would not seek out the embrace of the Church of Satan.

But what about the animal sacrifices, and even more horrible, the sacrificing of babies? The news reports of the Satanic Panic were crammed with these horror stories. Child sacrifice is said to be one of the gruesome trademarks of satanic ritual.

Except that no, actually, it's not, according to LaVey's *Satanic Bible*. He states unequivocally: "Under *no* circumstances would a Satanist sacrifice any animal or baby." The reason, again, is coldly, dispassionately logical. Children and animals are creatures that are still in touch with their wild, natural selves. Children haven't yet learned to govern their own self-indulgent tendencies, the way polite society insists that they do. Therefore, animals and children are revered in the satanic church, held up as an example for older (and more civilized) people to emulate.

Neither do Satanists sexually abuse children or animals. Again, it's a matter of innocence in the face of carnal lusts. Satanists are allowed and encouraged to indulge their physical desires, but *only* if it doesn't harm anyone else. Children are not capable of giving consent to sex. Therefore, to a true Satanist, child sexual abuse is strictly off-limits. It is, quite literally, against their religion. If a member of the Church of Satan abuses a child, sexually or otherwise, his membership is automatically terminated without the possibility of reinstatement.

Satanism is not about goat sacrifice and bloody upside-down crosses. It is about independent thought, about following one's physical desires. Obviously, it's not something everyone wants to follow. But a religious Satanist would not kidnap and murder children. Satanists don't even believe in Satan. They don't believe in any supernatural beings. Therefore, they don't perform sacrifices to those beings.

According to the FAQs on their website, Satanists are atheists. They see the universe as being supremely indifferent to human life. All values and rules for living, then, are subjective human constructs. "Satan" is simply a symbol of personal pride, liberty, and individuality. This does scare some people. It can be very unsettling, when you're used to a religion that says "Follow me," to see instead a religion that asks, "Where are you going?" Satanism says, think for yourself, and don't rely on outside sources for your own salvation.

There are, the website says, three basic types of satanic ritual. One is for compassion, for oneself and for others. Another is for lust, to release sexual urges. And one is for destruction, to cleanse oneself of anger towards someone who has done you an injustice.

This goes for the offshoot of Anton LaVey's Church of Satan, too, Michael Aquino's Temple of Set. This group takes as its focus the ancient Egyptian god Set, god of evil and darkness, mortal enemy of Osiris and Isis. Aquino writes of the difference between White and Black magic:

> *"White magic as practiced by primitive pagan and modern institutional religions offers devotees the illusion of 'reinclusion' in the universal scheme of things through ritualistic devotions and superstitions. The Black Magician on the other hand rejects both the desirability of union with the universe and any self-deceptive antics designed to create such an illusion. He has considered the existence of the individual psyche – the real you of the conscious intelligence – and has taken satisfaction from its existence as something unlike anything else in the universe. The Black Magician desires this psyche to live, to experience, to continue. He does not wish to die or to*

lose his consciousness and identity to a larger universal consciousness. He wants to be."

Aquino's book, *The Crystal Table of Set*, continues in much the same vein as LaVey's *Satanic Bible*. "The Temple of Set enjoys the colorful legacy of the Black Arts and we use many forms of Satanic imagery for our stimulation and pleasure. But we have not found that any interest or activity which an enlightened mature intellect would regard as undignified, sadistic, criminal or depraved is desirable, much less essential, to our work. Under no circumstance is any life form ever sacrificed or injured in a Black Magickal working of the Temple of Set. Violation of this rule will result in the offender's immediate expulsion and referral to law enforcement or animal protection authorities." The language is a bit clunky, but very clear.

That being said, there is a huge difference between religious Satanists and Devil-worshippers, or pseudo-Satanists. Devil-worshippers use the name of Satan for the shock value. These are the people who use the symbols of the occult as an actual religion, people who think they can summon demons by drawing sigils on basement floors and drinking blood. They may not be kidnapping children for use in their rites. They may not be sacrificing goats or slitting bulls' throats. They may not be saying the Mass backwards and using a naked woman as an altar. But they are open to the antisocial lure of evil. It's not Satanism, but it is demonic.

Teenagers who appear to be into Satan worship are something else entirely. Teens who use the trappings of Goth culture – black clothes, black fingernail polish, black-dyed spiky hair, even symbols like the upside-down cross – aren't necessarily into Satanism. They're using that symbolism not to worship Satan, but as a representation of their own nonconforming attitude. The message they're sending is one of rebelliousness, not Satanism. Odds are, they haven't read the Satanic Bible or embraced Satan as their Lord and master. Petty crime, or cemetery vandalism and desecration by teens, needs to be taken seriously and investigated seriously. But it should not automatically be labeled a satanic crime. (And why is it that, if a Catholic or Lutheran kid commits a crime, it's not labeled a "Christian ritual crime"?)

There's also some confusion in law enforcement circles about the difference between satanic activity and legend tripping. Legend tripping is a time-honored habit of some adventurous teens. Every community has a place hidden away from prying eyes (or maybe not so hidden), where a legend has sprung up. If you go to a certain cemetery at midnight, the spectral image of an irate farmer will appear and chase you away. Or you'll be able to hear organ music coming from a specific grave. Or if you sit on a stone chair that can be found in the middle of the dark woods, one of your friends will be dead within the year. The stories are endless, and endlessly fascinating. They draw teens, hungry for experience of the supernatural, like moths to a guttering flame. Graffiti, dead campfires, stubs of candles drippy with melted wax – most of this so-called evidence has perfectly reasonable explanations as the detritus of a gathering place for teens. Sometimes there are even more banal explanations. In New Hampshire, police claimed they had found animals that had been ritually slaughtered in the woods. As it turned out, the gruesome carcasses were simply roadkill that had been picked up by highway workers and dumped in the woods.

For most teenagers, whatever their beliefs regarding witchcraft, Wicca, Satanism or demons, the closest they will get to practicing witchcraft or Satanism is lighting up a stick of nag champa to make their room smell less funky. Previously, the word "witch" conjured up images of the Wicked Witch of the West, or the witch in Snow White – bent old crones with green skin and unfortunate choices in headwear. But modern witches are sexy. Modern witches are Alyssa Milano in *Charmed,* or Neve Campbell in *The Craft.* Who wants to emulate wicked witches when you have the glamorous team of Nicole Kidman and Sandra Bullock shining on the screen in *Practical Magic?* Witchcraft is becoming a social movement.

The Church of Satan is a scary thing for people to contemplate. For most people, the idea of a church devoted to the worship of the Big Bad is horrifying. Why would anyone in their right mind knowingly choose the dark side? And there are undoubtedly some unbalanced characters who call themselves Satanists for the shock value, or as a way to excuse reprehensible behavior. These are sick, disturbed people who really don't understand the philosophy of the *Satanic Bible.* They use Satanism as an excuse for doing the inexcusable.

The witch-hunters of the Renaissance took their job seriously. The *Malleus Maleficarum* is a work of deadly earnestness. It reads like a cross between an encyclopedia and an instruction manual for identifying and destroying witches. The question of demons and witchcraft was, for the Renaissance intellectual, a theme of scientific, as well as religious, importance. The *Malleus Maleficarum* is a finely detailed textbook of witch-hunting, filled with references to the Bible and many other theological writings.

In contrast, there was nothing remotely intellectual about the Satanic Panic. It wasn't even particularly religious in scope, beyond the obvious vaguely Christian fear of the Devil. Most of the investigators – therapists, FBI and other law enforcement officers, social workers – didn't have a strong religious affiliation themselves. They focused more on the child abuse angle of the case, rather than trying to prosecute people for their religious beliefs (which isn't allowed in America anyway). Even so, with absolutely zero physical evidence, the Panic eventually died down.

Satanism has been used as an excuse for all sorts of atrocities. The Satanic Panic was blown all out of proportion. But there have been horrible crimes committed in the name of Satan, just as there have been reprehensible acts committed in the name of Christ. Satan just gets all the bad press.

7. SPOOKY ACTION AT A DISTANCE: DEMONS IN SCIENCE

Science and religion have always had an uneasy relationship. Einstein was convinced that God had an important hand in science: "God does not play dice with the universe." Stephen Hawking, on the other hand, was more dismissive of the role of the Divine in science: "Not only does He play dice, sometimes he rolls the dice where He can't see."

When scientists started to explore the strange world of particle physics, they noticed that things at the subatomic level got really weird. The smaller a group you're measuring, the more unpredictable the behavior is. You can predict that a soccer mob will riot, but you can't predict what will happen to one person if he gets hit in the head with a brick.

Let's take a closer look at this. Radioactive nitrogen-13 has a half-life of ten minutes. This is a scientific fact. So if you start out with a pound of it, after ten minutes, half of the particles will have decayed. That's what the half-life of an element is. You'll have eight ounces of nitrogen-13 that is radioactive, and eight ounces that aren't. After ten more minutes, you'll have four ounces that are radioactive, and twelve ounces that aren't, and so on and so on. As time goes by, you'll keep getting more and more of the element that has decayed, down to one ounce that's still radioactive and fifteen ounces that's not. But here's the weird thing – that chunk of element will never completely decay. It will keep getting halved, and halved again. And when it gets down to halving tiny bits of stuff, whether or not a particle will remain radioactive gets impossible to predict.

The odds of any particle decaying within that ten minute half-life are exactly fifty-fifty, whether it's part of the original pound of stuff, or if you're down to an eighth of an ounce. And the odds *stay* at fifty-fifty, for all the particles, whether it's right away or at any time during those ten minutes. This is also a scientific fact. The decay of a large amount of an element can be predicted; that's where we get the concept of a half-life. But there is no way to predict the degradation of one particle. The material itself will definitely be half as radioactive after a fixed amount of time. But it's impossible to predict which particle will or will not be radioactive.

Newtonian physics can be used to predict anything from the fall of a ripe apple to the movement of the galaxies. But those explanations become useless at the subatomic level. When you get down to a certain size, Newtonian physics no longer apply.

Consider Schroedinger's poor, (possibly) doomed cat. The cat is trapped in a box with a bottle of poison. There's also one particle of an element in there that will decay

– and if it does, the poison will be released and the cat will die. But since there's no way to predict whether or not a particle will decay, we have no idea if the cat is dead or alive until we open the box. So until that box is opened, *the cat exists in two universes*, right there in front of you. The cat is both dead *and* alive until you look at it. Then, as soon as you check it, the other cat ceases to exist. If the cat's alive, you've just destroyed the dead cat.

This is some weird stuff. Looking at quantum physics almost involves a return to the mindset of the Middle Ages: if you can't observe it, it's not part of the natural world. It's just … bizarre. As a kind of shorthand, physicists started using demons to explain the behavior of these particles.

We think of space as being, well, spacious. If I am over here and you are over there, I have to cross a certain amount of space in order to interact with you. I have to walk across a room, or jog across a field, in order to tap you on the shoulder to get your attention. Even if I just stand at one end of the room, or the field, and yell, the air molecules jostle each other, transferring the energy down the line, until a few of them bump into your eardrums and convey the sound of my voice.

But quantum physics says that this space isn't a separation at all.

One of the weirdest parts of quantum physics describes something called "quantum entanglement" – what Einstein called "spooky action at a distance." Basically, there are two particles that are created at the same place and time. Even if those particles are later separated in space, an action on one of them can have the same effect on the other one, no matter how far apart they are. Weird as it may seem, just because objects are apart from each other in space, that doesn't necessarily mean they are separate. Somehow, they are joined, with a bizarre sense of awareness. If you tickle one particle, the other one laughs.

Sounds like voodoo, doesn't it? That's why Einstein called it spooky.

The idea of "demons" became a placeholder to explain fundamentals of particle physics. It was easier to visualize these unknowable particles by saying, "Okay, so we have this quark over here, and a demon is riding on it, so it always spins clockwise. And over there, there's another quark that's also spinning clockwise, because the demon's twin brother is riding that one. Two different particles, however far apart, are moving and acting in the exact same way. Why? Well … let's say because a demon and his twin are riding each particle."

Again, just as with the Europeans naming places in the American wilderness, if it's weird or strange, we'll call it by the name demon. And that way, if the science turns out to be something of unimaginable potency, we won't have the Church picketing our labs because we attributed this to angels – but blaming it on demons is perfectly acceptable.

Louis Slotin, a Canadian scientist, died while working on the Manhattan Project. He accidentally dropped a hemisphere of beryllium onto a plutonium core; witnesses saw a glowing blue light and felt a blast of heat. Slotin died nine days later of acute radiation poisoning. Slotin was the second casualty – his accident followed the death of Harry Daghlian, who had been exposed to radiation from the same core that killed Slotin. The plutonium was later nicknamed "the demon core."

Demons are the perfect way to explain particle physics precisely because they don't have to obey our laws of time and physics and space. Douglas Adams knew this. In his Dirk Gently detective books, he wrote a locked-room mystery in which the perpetrator was an eight foot tall furry monster hiding behind an air molecule.

We no longer blame sour milk on witches acting in concert with the Devil. We know that disease isn't the work of demons. The invisible has become visible. Our experience of the world hasn't changed; just our perception of it. We still get sick, but now we know enough to follow a few simple rules: wash your hands, don't eat stuff you find on the sidewalk, don't lick doorknobs. We can use microscopes to pry open the secrets of the unseen world …but for all our knowledge, there are things that remain unseen, outside our newly sharpened perception. We can write our names on the head of a pin, but we still haven't caught any angels doing the Macarena. We know about magnetism, and radio waves, and gravity, and EMF energy – but we still don't have any concrete proof of ghosts, or demons, or angels. The mighty djinn of the Arabian Nights have been watered down into the form of a pretty blonde in pastel harem pants.

We have a lot more evidence for the existence of germs than we do for the existence of demons. Yet how many people do you know that, while throwing a pinch of spilled salt over their left shoulder to hit the Devil in the eye, will still follow the five second rule in the kitchen?

8. THE MAGIC LAMP: WESTERN VS EASTERN ATTITUDES TOWARD DEMONS

In Western thought, demons attack people for good reasons. People become possessed because they open themselves up to possession by monkeying around with the occult. Or they are devout Christians, and the Devil wants to make an example of them by making them suffer. But on the other side of the world, things are very different. Demons are everywhere, but one doesn't have to be particularly righteous or craven to attract their attention. In the East, you can just be walking down the street, minding your own business, and get jumped by a demon. Happens all the time.

Basically, the attitude of demons in Eastern thought seems to be "hey, it's nothing personal."

We find this hard to swallow, in the West. But it permeates the Eastern consciousness, creeping into daily life all the time. One of the most delightful examples of this comes from the "creative translation" in a Honda motorcycle owner's manual from 1962.

After World War II, a lot of people in war-ravaged European cities were getting around on bicycles. In the next couple of decades, motor companies started putting small engines on these bicycles, turning them into nimble little motorcycles. Companies like Honda and Kawasaki in Japan and Ducati in Italy started turning out these smaller-sized motorbikes. America, with its long distances, had been churning out big bikes like Harleys and Indians. But the Japanese and Italians found a ready market in the United States for their smaller, more affordable bikes. In 1962, Honda provided a helpful English translation of their manual.

1962 Safety Rules From Honda:

1. *At the rise of hand by Policeman, stop rapidly.*
2. *When a passenger of the foot hooves in sight, tootel the horn trumpet melodiously at first. If he still obstacles your passage, tootel him with vigor and express by word of mouth, warning Hi, hi.*
3. *Beware of the wandering horse that he shall not take fright as you pass him. Do not explode the exhaust box at him. Go soothingly by.*
4. *Give big space to the festive dog that makes sport in roadway. Avoid entanglement of dog with wheel spokes.*
5. *Go soothingly on the grease mud, for there lurks the skid demon! Press the brake foot as you roll around the corners, and save the collapse and tie up.*

In addition to being lovely in their imagery, these rules reveal something interesting about the Asian character. Avoid the mud, because there's a demon lurking there, and there's a possibility it will attack you. So just stay away from it, and you should be fine. But if you put yourself in that situation, you open yourself up to demonic influence. It's a great way to save face, which is paramount in Asian culture. I know there's a demon in that grease-slicked mud on the road. If I wipe out, it's not my fault. It's not anything I did wrong, it's just that, well, the demon got me.

In Islam, the devil's name is Iblis. He is the father of the djinn, able to assume any form. Iblis got into trouble with Allah, just as Satan did with God. Again, it was over the situation of Adam.

When Allah created Adam, he ordered all of the angels to bow down and worship his new creation. Iblis, who like the djinn was created from smokeless fire, refused.

He claimed that a being of fire should not be required to worship a being of dust. Allah cursed Iblis for his pride and threw him out of paradise. He allowed Iblis to roam the earth, tempting humans and destroying those who yielded. Iblis can't force humans to sin; he can only tempt them to make that choice.

In the Sufi tradition, Iblis refused to bow to Adam because he could only bow to God. Therefore, Iblis is revered for his loyalty and devotion. He is seen as a noble figure who would rather be separated from God than be united with God against God's will.

Djinns are a force of the natural world, rather than being strictly evil. We can think of djinns as being sort of like, oh, gunpowder, as an example. You can use gunpowder to blast a hole through a mountainside, to make travel through the mountains easier. Or you can use it to make cannonballs and blow bridges to smithereens.

In the stories of *The Arabian Nights*, djinns are very powerful beings that humans have managed to harness. Their power is immense, but it is under the control of the human hero or villain. Humans can order a djinn to build a palace in a day, or bring the hero fabulous riches. Or, if the djinn falls into the wrong hands, its power can be used against the hero. That marvelous palace can be whisked away to another country overnight, leaving the hero homeless and destitute. No matter who is rubbing the lamp, though, the djinn is bound to obey.

In these stories, we see the Eastern mindset at work. The djinns are not inherently evil, nor are they inherently good. They are, to borrow a phrase from modern gaming culture, chaotic neutral. It is the intentions of the humans controlling the djinn that dictate the djinn's actions. The djinn, although enormously powerful, is bound to its human master's will. It is the human that uses the djinn's power for good or evil.

Just as in Christian theology, there are different levels of djinn possession. Being touched by a djinn is not as severe as full possession. When a human is touched by a djinn, the djinn enters the human, but leaves whenever it wants to. The djinn annoys the human by making him or her feel uncomfortable, distressed, or depressed without any obvious reason. The djinn can cause headaches or other pains, nightmares, insomnia, or loss of appetite. These troubles come and go when the djinn does.

The djinn causing the problems may not even be evil. He might just be upset because the human may have slighted or insulted him, stepped on his toe, threw boiling water out of a window onto him, or threw a stone at him (in the djinn's guise as a black cat or dog). The djinn takes revenge on the human by tormenting his victim.

Since djinn are known to take on a reptilian form, sometimes manifesting as half-human, half-snake, with clawed hands and snakelike eyes, Muhammad cautioned his followers to be careful about evicting snakes from their houses. After all, a snake could very well be a djinn in disguise, and killing one outright could make its relatives take revenge. A snake inside a house should be asked three times to leave.

If the snake ignored the request, it was probably actually a snake, and not a djinn, so it was fine to kill it.

Djinn possession is much more severe. A djinn in full possession of a human will never leave unless chased out by force. There are two kinds of djinns that possess humans. One type is completely evil, out to harm humans in any way possible. There vengeful, nasty sprits constantly cause pain, illness, and confusion to their host.

The other type, oddly enough, isn't malicious. Djinns sometimes fall in love with humans, and wait for a moment of weakness to slip into the body to be as close as possible to his or her beloved. Luckily, djinn lovers usually don't harm their human host unless they are upset by something the human does.

Full possession happens when a djinn takes over both a human's body and mind. This state is temporary, and it leaves the human victim unable to remember exactly what happened during the possession. Many times, the human is completely oblivious to the fact that a djinn was directing his voice and his movements.

The state of full possession is different for different humans. A healer will sometimes read from the Koran – the Word – to force the djinn to appear in a controlled form. Other djinns respond well to music and drumming, as in the zar rituals. A specific drum rhythm is combined with music to draw out the djinn, and each djinn has its own song.

Some Egyptians feel that they have a devil on their shoulder, whispering to them, talking them into misbehaving. People who are possessed by a djinn often complain of actually hearing these whispers. Some describe it as actual voices, while others hear a whistling sound that drives them to distraction. If a djinn is stronger than the human it possesses, it can control the human, making its victim dance in the street, scream, cry, or even laugh uncontrollably, or tear off his or her clothes.

When the human does something to upset the djinn, the djinn takes over. Sometimes, the possession is brought on by anger – when a possessed person gets angry, out comes the djinn, directing the human's words and actions.

Interestingly, full djinn possession in the Middle East isn't necessarily connected to any moral or spiritual failing on the part of the possessed. In Western culture, full possession has to be invited, by things such as intense interest in the occult, excessive use of a Ouija board, or the practice of black magic. But a human can run afoul of a djinn simply by going about daily life. A djinn can even fall in love with a human and move right on in – and there's nothing the human can do about that.

The truly evil djinns do seem to take special delight in possessing the pious faithful. This echoes the early Christian tradition in which saints were tormented by demons.

Some people have claimed to have djinns that served them, rather than possessed them. This service wasn't based on the humans' controlling the djinn, as Aladdin did with the lamp, but on the love and devotion their invisible companion felt for them. Some men in Cairo arrange to marry a female djinn so they can satisfy their needs until they can afford to marry a human girl. These marriages seem to work out well, but no one really knows ... a man who marries a djinn is forbidden to speak of his marriage, for fear of inflaming the jealousy of his invisible wife.

Several people have said that djinns live much the same way humans do, eating and drinking alongside humans at the same table. This is why, they say, it's important to bless the food with the name of Allah before a meal. Without this precaution, the djinns will eat the essence of the food, stealing it from the humans and leaving the food devoid of nutrition.

Many Egyptians agree that djinns live much longer than humans, up to thousands of years. Some feel that digging for pharaonic treasures is dangerous, that the ancient graves are protected by the djinns. They say that djinns are bound to the tombs, and will punish anyone who violates the sacred place, even five thousand years later. They point to the strange series of calamities that followed the opening of Tutankhamen's tomb, and nod knowingly.

Whether djinns have evil intentions or are just chaotic energy, they are always considered potentially harmful and difficult to control. Djinns are made of fire. If a fire is not contained, it will burn and destroy.

But just as fire can be used positively if it's controlled, djinns are seen to be evil if left to their own devices, but can be useful to humans. Djinns are unpredictable and untrustworthy because they make no distinction between good and evil. They are outside of any human view of morality. Many djinn are not evil of themselves – they're just very chaotic. Djinns are capable of loving and caring for humans, but their love is passionate, tempestuous.

This is not to say that Middle Eastern culture is completely credulous when it comes to tales of djinn possession. Barbara Drieskins, the author of *Living With Djinns*, met a pharmacist in Cairo who helped many people who had trouble with djinns. He admitted, though, that about ninety percent of possession cases, especially those involving women, were fake. He explained that many women who complained of possession were living in wretched circumstances, and couldn't see any good way out of their situation.

"Whenever he saw one of them approaching, he thought to himself, 'Here comes another one suffering from mother-in-law sickness.' Because many of them were living with their husband's mother, they lived in a state of constant tension. They had no one to talk to, and if they complained to their husband, it only made the situation worse. So when words could not help they found another way of expressing themselves: through nightmares, dizziness, loss of appetite and pains, and other typical complaints of possession."

But even this hard-headed doctor believed that djinns and possession did exist – just not in every case where someone claimed to be possessed. "The question is," the pharmacist told the author, "what to do as a healer when you are confronted with such a case? I could tell her that there is nothing wrong with her and that she only needs to change her life, but often these women do not have the means to change. Or I could give her the chance to express her complaints through the idiom of possession. These women always bring their husbands or their sisters-in-law or even their mothers-in-law with them. When I call up the spirit, it is the spirit who voices her despair and who formulates some of her demands. In these cases, both the patient and I know that we are playing a game, but often this game is a very serious one: it is her only way out and then I do not consider it my duty to tell this little secret to anybody."

But Egyptian women have a secret weapon. In modern Muslim culture, a curious (and liberating) belief has survived the passage of years. The zar is a djinn that attacks women, possessing them, and refusing to leave until the victim had gotten an acceptably lavish assortment of presents from her husband. Rosemary Ellen Guiley, in her *Encyclopedia of Demons and Demonology*, writes: "Second-class citizens under male domination, Muslim women depend on the zar to give them some measure of power and privilege. Husbands must provide expensive gifts (jewelry, perfume, clothes) and sweetmeats to create peace in the household. Such appeasement raises suspicions of manipulation, but so ingrained in Islamic culture is the belief in spirit interference that husbands dare not tempt fate."

This is fascinating. Here we have a culture that treats women like inferior beings. In everyday life, a woman who speaks up for herself is liable to find herself slapped down, or worse, stoned or beheaded. But this culture also has something just as alien to us as the idea of killing a woman for being independent – it has the zar. It gives women, the silent, faceless masses hidden behind burqas, an immense amount of carefully directed power.

Zar exorcisms are still held today, even in cosmopolitan cities like Cairo. "Women from all walks of life participate, whirling and dancing until the spirit leaves them and they return home, exhausted but entertained. Relief may only be temporary, and it may return with another infraction committed by a husband. Men are expected to believe in the possession, which, in addition to giving women the freedom to ask for gifts, permits them to scold and upbraid their husbands in a manner that would be forbidden under normal circumstances" (Guiley).

This is a healing ritual, reconciling the patient with the djinn that possesses her. These rituals consist of sacrifice, music, dance, and trance. There are individual zars organized for a particular patient that can be very elaborate. There are also collective zar rituals, usually weekly. These are simplified, and open to the public.

The zar is not limited to Egypt. It can be found all over the Middle East. In East Africa, not too geographically distant from Egypt, there is a malady that primarily affects women called the mpepo sickness. The description of this sounds remarkably like zar possession. The mpepo sickness is characterized by abnormal eagerness for food, brightly-colored clothing, other adornments, and pepper and other strong condiments. Sometimes the suffering woman is seized by a fit of rage and goes into convulsions. She dances to the rhythm of the mpepo drum until she collapses with exhaustion. Only then does she seem to find some relief. Mpepo sickness is considered a noble and distinguished affliction.

In Mecca, a researcher found that the zar ritual had become practically epidemic, with most of the women of the area being affected. In 1889, the researcher Snouck Hurgronje wrote that the zar ritual had become a sort of pastime for the women of Mecca.

"The fight with the Zar displays at once the darkest and the happiest side of the Meccan women's life ... From infancy they hear so much talk of the Zar that any specific maladies which overtake them generally appear as the domination of a Zar ... the Zar declares himself ready to depart on a certain day with the usual ceremonies, if in the interim certain stipulations have been fulfilled. He demands a new and beautiful garment, gold or silver trinkets, etc. As he himself is hidden from all human perception, nothing can be done except carry out his wish and make gifts of the specified objects to the sick body which he inhabits; it is touching to see how these evil spirits take into account the age, tastes, and needs of the possessed." (There's more than a bit of Euro-centric snark in that last sentence.)

Some modern Egyptians look down on stories of djinns, especially those involving the zar ritual. They see them as a way for women to manipulate their husbands, or as an excuse to give in to the temptations of alcohol or cigarettes. (We say, "the devil made me do it." In Muslim culture, a djinn is responsible.) Zar is seen, sometimes, as psychodrama. The women suffering from djinn possession are seen as hopelessly old-fashioned at best, and at worst, weak and foolish.

But djinn possession is still a real thing, especially in Egypt. Drieskins, who spent years in Cairo studying the djinn in folklore and in everyday life, interviewed several women who felt they were possessed by djinns. One of them, Sakaya, showed up to her second interview with one side of her face swollen and bruised. She explained that the spirits had hit her because she had revealed their secrets in her first meeting with the author.

Islam has two very distinct ways of dealing with the djinns that attack the faithful. The Word of the Koran separates the world of humans and the world of spirits. Thus, when the Koran is invoked, it puts strict limits on the djinns' presence and influence.

An Egyptian newspaper published an account of a man who had a female djinn fall in love with him. She loved the man so much that, at his request, she possessed the daughter of one of his neighbors. The girl went to a wise man for help. By using rational arguments based on the Koran, the wise man was able to convince the djinn that she had made a mistake – Allah ordered djinns not to harm humans or to ally themselves with people who intend harm. By pointing this out, the wise man used logic to talk the djinn into leaving the girl's body.

Using the Koran to heal a person of a djinn's influence is a form of healing by separation, a bit like the Christian technique of exorcism. The spirit is required to exit the body of the possessed person, and leave the sufferer in peace. But Middle Eastern folk custom also recognizes another form of relief, a healing through reconciliation. The zar ritual is just the most extreme version of this. The goal of these rituals is not to create any distance between the human and the possessing spirit, but to satisfy the djinn so that djinn and human can coexist in peace. These rituals don't involve the reading of the Koran. Instead, they focus on music and songs, and poems of love, sorrow, and passion. It's a kinder, gentler way of dealing with a possessing spirit.

9. ONCE UPON A TIME: DEMON TALES

American folklore is peppered with stories about the Devil. Quite often these tales have heroes who trick the Devil into giving them years more life when he comes for their soul. Actually, these characters are more anti-heroes than heroes – the reason the Devil shows up for them in the first place is because these folks have lived lives of petty wickedness.

When the Devil shows up to collect the fellow's soul, the hero will resort to trickery, trapping the Devil, and letting him go only in return for ten more years of life. The hero will outsmart the Devil by asking him to climb a tree to get some apples, then carving a cross into the bark, or having him sit in a chair that traps him. A particularly ingenious trick is to suggest the Devil turn himself into a dime. The plan is that the hero will use the dime to buy himself and the Devil a cold one, to drink as they walk the dusty road to Hell. The Devil can then transform into a moth and escape the till. But when the Devil turns himself into a dime, the hero pops him into his coin purse, which has a cross on it. The Devil is trapped yet again.

These "trapping the devil" stories usually end with the hero dying of old age. His soul goes first to Heaven, but he is refused admittance, because he has made a deal with the Devil. (Sometimes, if he used the old coin purse trick, he's still got the Devil in his pocket.) Denied Heaven, the hero then tries to get into Hell, but the Devil, knowing he's a troublemaker, won't let him in. The hero is forced to wander the earth forever.

German gypsies have a lovely story to explain why a horseshoe is considered good luck. Horses are intensely important in the nomadic gypsy culture, so anything associated with them is good luck right from the jump. Gypsies are consummate horse traders, so horses are emblems not only of mobility but also of livelihood, even prosperity. Horseshoes are traditionally made of iron, which is pretty much universally seen as a powerful weapon against evil spirits. But the gypsies of Germany have gone a little further in their explanation.

Long ago, there were four demons called Bad Luck, Bad Health, Unhappiness, and Death. One day while out riding, a gypsy chief was attacked by the demon Bad Luck. The chief whipped his horse to a lather to escape the demon. In its headlong flight, the horse threw a shoe, which struck Bad Luck in the forehead, killing it stone dead. The chief reined in his horse, and went back and picked up the thrown horseshoe. He nailed the shoe to the outside of his caravan, right by the door.

When the other three demons heard of Bad Luck's death, they came hunting for the young gypsy. When they got to the caravan, though, they saw the iron horseshoe that had killed Bad Luck hanging next to the door. Remembering that the horse had three remaining shoes, the demons fled, frightened for their lives. From that day on, a horseshoe has been seen as a talisman against the four demons of Bad Luck, Unhappiness, Bad Health, and Death.

Romanian gypsy brides hold a coin under their left arm during the wedding ceremony. As the couple leaves the church, the bride secretly lets the coin drop to the ground, as a payment to the Devil for protection for the marriage. Whoever finds the coin later is entitled to seven years of good luck.

The culture of Portugal is a heady mix of Spanish and Moor. Many of the folktales of Portugal are versions of stories familiar in other European countries – Cinderella, Snow White and Rose Red, and Hansel and Gretel. But others are unique to that country. One of these stories is a wise little tale called "The Price of Eggs."

A young man was about to set sail on a journey when he passed an inn and stopped in for a bite to eat. The mistress of the inn said that all she had to offer were some boiled eggs. The young man ordered a copper's worth. After eating, he gave the innkeeper a cruzado and asked for change.

"I don't have any change. Just pay me when you come this way again," she said.

The young man traveled far and wide, and he often passed shrines on the road. Whenever he saw such a shrine, he would stop and make a small donation for the souls of the dead in purgatory. These shrines were covered in pictures depicting Christ and the saints, the souls of the dead facing judgment, and the Devil. The young man would speak aloud as he made his donation. "Here, souls of the dead, here's money for you, so that you will give me aid. And you, devil, don't help me, but don't hinder me either."

Several years later, the young man returned home. The first stop he made was to the inn where he had eaten the eggs.

"I've come to pay my debt," he told the innkeeper.

"What debt is that?" she asked.

"When I left town, I stopped in here and ate a copper's worth of eggs and did not pay for them."

"Oh, now I remember," the innkeeper said. "And you think you can pay off that debt with only a copper? You ate six eggs, yes? Just let me figure out what you really owe me. Six eggs would have hatched into six hens, and their eggs would have hatched too, and it's been so many years ..." The woman continued to count until the bill added up to several hundred milreis.

The young man didn't have nearly enough money to pay this huge sum, so he was taken to prison.

While the young man was in prison, a stranger came to visit him in his cell. "You have no one to defend you? I'll do it. Today at three they will sentence you. I will be your lawyer and come to defend you."

That afternoon the young man was taken into court. The mistress of the inn was there also. At three o'clock the stranger who was to defend the young man showed up in court, his face black with soot. The judge frowned.

"Why didn't you wash your face before coming into court?"

"Because I was roasting chestnuts to sow in the ground," the young man's lawyer answered.

The mistress of the inn interrupted with a scornful laugh. "Chestnut trees can't grow from roasted chestnuts, you idiot."

"And chickens can't hatch from boiled eggs," the lawyer shot back. Turning to the judge, he said, "This young man does not owe the innkeeper as much money as she says he does. She asks that he pay for chickens she would have raised from boiled eggs. Let him go free."

The judge agreed, and the young man was free to go. And who was the lawyer? The devil, of course.

> To protect yourself against the Devil, hang a mirror on your porch by the door. The Devil is very vain, and will spend the entire night admiring himself in the mirror. He'll waste hours there, until the sun rises and he's forced to go back to Hell.

African culture has plenty of demon tales. Here's one:

If you go to Guyana, you may run across a demon called a baccoo. It's a little man in a bottle, like a genie. This demon will help you get anything – women, money, power – anything. They say politicians like baccoo. Trouble is, it's very hard to get rid of one, because after all, who wants to live in a bottle?

If you let a baccoo out of its bottle, you have to feed it banana and milk, or it will haunt you. This haunting is much like poltergeist behavior – furniture moving, picture breaking, big stone falling on your roof.

So if you ever go to Guyana, and you see a bottle on the ground, don't pick it up. Otherwise you gonna hear somebody say, "T'ank you very much!"

Another African story is a time-honored Jack tale. Jack and the Devil were arguing about who was the strongest. The Devil picked up a mule. Well, Jack picked up that same mule. The Devil pulled up a tree by its roots. Jack pulled up one just as big. The Devil broke an anchor cable. So did Jack.

The Devil lost patience and snorted, "Shucks! Dis ain't no sho' nuff trial. Dis is chillun's foolishness. Meet me out in dat hund'ed acre clearin' tomorrow mornin' at nine o'clock. We'll see who kin throw mah hammer de furtherest. De one do dat is de strongest."

Jack said, "Dat suits me."

Next day, the Devil showed up with his hammer, which was bigger than a church. A crowd gathered at the field to see the contest. Jack rode up on a horse and said, "We'se all heah, so le's git to it. Who goin' first?"

The Devil said, "Me. Everybody stand back and gimme room."

The Devil swung that hammer round and round, then let go. The hammer went clean out of sight. "Is Tuesday now," the Devil said. "Y'all go home and come back Thursday morning at nine. It ain't gonna fall 'til then."

Well, everyone showed back up on Thursday morning. The hammer did fall with a bang – made a hole as big as Polk County.

Now it was Jack's turn. He picked that hammer up and he hefted it, to get a feel for it. Then he looked up at the sky and yelled, "Move over, Gabriel! Look out, Raphael! You better stand way back, Jesus! Ah'm fixin' to throw!"

The Devil run up to Jack and he says "Now hold on dere a minute! Don't you throw mah damn hammer up dere! Ah left a whole lot of mah tools up dere when dey put me out, and Ah ain't got 'em back yet. Don't you throw mah hammer up dere too!"

The Sukasaptati, or Seventy Tales of the Parrot, is a collection of Sanskrit stories from the Hindu tradition. The stories are told to a woman by her pet parrot, one per night over the course of several months – much like the tales of Scheherezade in the Arabian Nights. The woman's husband is off on a trip, and the parrot is trying to keep the woman from going out to meet her lover. One of the tales involves a demon who has to be driven out not once, but twice.

Once upon a time there was a man named Kecava who was wise, but poor. He had a wife called Karagara, or Poison-giver, who was a vicious hag. She treated everyone around her so horribly that even the demon which lived in Kecava's house fled into the desert just to get away from Karagara. After years of this torment, Kecava finally left his wife.

The demon which had lived in Kecava's house saw him walking along, and said, "Kecava, I want to do a favor for you." Kecava was afraid of the demon, but the demon reassured him. "I used to live in your house, but I left because of Karagara's abuse. Since you were essentially my landlord for so many years, I'd like to repay you.

"Go to the village of Mrigavati. I will go there too, and I'll take possession of the princess. I won't let myself be driven out by any exorcist until you get there. Then, I'll go as soon as you tell me to."

Kecava arrived at the village and heard the heralds telling the news that the princess was possessed and needed help. Her father, King Madana, had promised the princess' hand in marriage to anyone who could cure her of her demonic affliction. Kecava went to the palace and offered to drive out the demon. He prayed and burned incense, but the demon refused to leave. Finally, Kecava cried out, "In the name of Karagara, come forth!" The demon replied, "You win – I'm coming out!" The demon left the princess immediately. The king was so grateful that he gave Kecava half of his kingdom and the princess in marriage.

The demon then went to the town of Karnavati and possessed the queen, who was the princess' aunt. The demon tormented the queen unmercifully, and she wasted away nearly to a skeleton. Her husband, the king, sent a messenger to King Madana and begged him to send the magician Kecava to the palace to help the queen.

Kecava went to Karnavati and asked to see the possessed queen. When he was taken to her, the demon taunted him, saying, "Ha! I've done your bidding once. I'm not going anywhere."

Hearing this, Kecava realized the demon was the same one that had possessed his wife. He leaned close to the queen's ear and whispered, "Oh, I just wanted to warn you that Karagara followed me here, and she's right outside the door."

The demon, terrified at the thought of meeting Karagara again, left the queen immediately. The king showered Kecava with riches, and he went back to his home and his new wife.

According to Vedic tradition, gods (devas) and demons (asuras) were created by the same entity. Asuras are not necessarily evil – sometimes they are quite devout, within the context of the Hindu religion.

Sometimes, the Hindu gods have to work for their immortality. The gods decided to create more amrita, the nectar of everlasting life. To do this, they had to churn the Ocean of Milk. They did this using a snake wrapped around Mount Meru, balanced on a turtle. One end of the snake was pulled by gods, the other end, by demons. When the amrita was finished, the gods and the demons fought over who should be allowed to have it. (The gods won.)

Chicago at the turn of the last century was a vibrant, noisy, dirty hodgepodge of cultures. People came to the toddlin' town from all over Europe and beyond, seeking their fortune and a new life in the Windy City.

They found new lives, at least. Communities sprang up in the dirty streets – Little Italy, Chinatown, islands of Hispanic and Czech and German immigrants. Some of the younger transplants thrived in the new soil of America. The older ones, though, often found themselves trapped within a barrier of language and deep-seated customs. They came to the expansive New World only to live cramped, insulated lives in the heart of a big city, limited by language and habit to interaction only within their own communities.

But there was a bright spot in this gritty existence, a spark of light and hope in the dirty streets that often stank of garbage, horse manure, train exhaust, and failed dreams.

It was the brain child of a lonely little girl, and it was called Hull House.

Jane Addams grew up with a powerful sense of responsibility for those less fortunate than she was. She described herself, in her autobiography, as "an ugly, pigeon-toed little girl" who longed to help the poor. When she was not yet seven years old, she went with her father to visit his mill. The mill was next to the poorest quarter in the town. Little Jane "declared with much firmness when I grew up I should of course, have a large house, but it would not be built among the other large houses, but right in the midst of horrid little houses like these."

When she grew up, she went to college and became a social worker. She finally had the means to make that childhood dream come true. She and another social worker, Ellen Gates Starr, started a settlement house in 1889 to provide food and shelter for the poor of Chicago. The women found a massive building at 800 South Halsted Street, and leased it from the owner, a Miss Helen Culver. It had been built in 1856 for one of Chicago's pioneer citizens, Charles J. Hull. The neighborhood had once been a fashionable address, but after the Chicago Fire in 1871, the wealthy moved away to other areas of the city. The Near West Side became a haven for Italian, Greek, Irish, German, Bohemian, and Russian and Polish Jewish immigrants. The building had already seen several decades of life, serving variously as a second hand furniture store, and as a home for the aged run by the Little Sisters of the Poor.

Addams and her staff set about trying to make life in Chicago easier for the immigrant population of the Near West Side. "We early found ourselves spending many hours in efforts to secure support for deserted women, insurance for bewildered widows, damages for injured operators, furniture from the clutches of the installment store." She often compared Hull House to a big brother whose mere presence on the playground protects the little ones from bullies.

One oddity that Addams noticed when she and her assistants moved in was that the tenants in the house insisted on keeping a pail of water on the attic stairs. When asked about this curious habit, the second-floor tenants could only mumble something about ghosts not being able to cross running water. Addams admitted that her interpretation could simply have been her own eagerness for finding folklore. But not even the healthiest appetite for strange stories could have prepared Addams for the weirdness that would soon descend on Hull House – a weirdness that survives in legend to this day.

In the summer of 1913, Addams and her staff began to get a sharp increase in the number of visitors to Hull House, many of whom were elderly immigrant women. These women came from wildly varying cultures and neighborhoods, but they all converged on Hull House with the same grim purpose.

They were there, they all said, to see the Devil Baby.

Addams and her staff were taken aback by this odd request. There was not, and had never been, a devil baby at Hull House, they said with complete assurance. But the visitors were adamant. They insisted that a neighborhood family had recently been cursed with the birth of a demonic child. The baby, they said, had been born sporting horns and a tail, sometimes even cloven hoofs, and roundly cursing its parents. Some versions even stuck a foul-smelling cigar in the infant's mouth.

The origin of this frightful creature varied, according to who was telling the story. Interestingly, each of the immigrant groups had a different interpretation of the infant's supposed origin. Italian women said that a good Catholic woman had hung a picture of the Virgin Mary on the wall of her apartment, and her atheist husband had snarled that he would rather have the devil in the house than a picture of the Blessed Virgin on the wall. Jewish visitors to Hull House told a different tale. In this version, a married couple already had a house full of girls. The husband, desperately wanting a son this time around, swore that he'd rather have the devil in his house than another daughter. Still others insisted that the trouble had started even before the wife's pregnancy, when an immigrant couple had gone before a priest with the intention of getting married. The bride, in all innocence, had spoken her vows, but the groom came to the ceremony with unconfessed sins in his shady past. This lapse was reflected in the hideous appearance of their firstborn child. All of the stories boiled down to the same moral lesson: the baby's father was being punished, either for his ingratitude for the blessed event or for mistreatment of the expectant mother.

It is a silent testament to Addams' influence on her neighborhood that in every version of the story, the despairing father breaks down and brings the demon infant to Hull House for her to deal with. Workers at the house allegedly took the demon child to a local church for baptism, but the baby wriggled free from the priest's hands and danced along the pews, chortling madly. Addams is said to have locked the baby in an upstairs bedroom at the house, where it would be seen peering down with a horrible expression at the life going on in the streets below, a life it was forbidden to share. The baby, according to legend, eventually died, leaving behind no sign of its existence but the stories that swirled around Hull House ever after.

Jane Addams devoted thirty pages of her book *The Second Twenty Years at Hull House* to this story, and her compassionate interpretation of the circumstances that led to the tale's creation. She writes that it all began with three Italian women rushing in to Hull House, describing the Devil Baby (in the first iteration of the story), and demanding to see it. For the next six weeks, she says, it was pretty much the only topic of conversation in the settlement house.

"For six weeks as I went about the house I would hear a voice at the telephone repeated for the hundredth time that day, 'No, there is no such baby'; 'No, we never had it here'; 'No, he couldn't have seen it for fifty cents'; 'We didn't send it anywhere, because we never had it'; 'I don't mean to say that your sister-in-law lied, but there must be some mistake'; 'There is no use getting up an excursion from Milwaukee, for there isn't any Devil Baby at Hull House'; 'We can't give reduced rates, because we are not exhibiting anything'; and so on and on." Her bemusement quickly turned to irritation with the throngs clamoring to see the demonic infant. The one group that did have her sympathy was elderly ladies.

Addams was deeply invested in the immigrant population she served at Hull House. After six weeks of a constant parade of women asking to see the Devil Baby, Addams realized that there was a theme to these requests. She became aware that the story was serving the need of these women to tell a tale and to be heard. This was a chance to win the respect of their neighbors and family.

Addams used this strange situation as a springboard to share the plight of immigrant women. In the October 1916 issue of *Atlantic Monthly*, she wrote that "the old women who came to visit the Devil Baby believed that the story would secure them a hearing at home ... and as they prepared themselves with every detail of it, their old faces shone with a timid satisfaction." Women came to see the demonic child, and stayed to tell Addams of their own tribulations.

"Because the Devil Baby embodied an undeserved wrong to a poor mother, whose tender child had been claimed by the forces of evil, his merely reputed presence had power to attract to Hull House hundreds of women who had been humbled and disgraced." They realized they had a companion in the harried mother. Her problems were their problems. Maybe they didn't have a Devil Baby of their own, but they had hardships at home all the same.

Going to Hull House in search of the Devil Baby not only gave these women the opportunity to get out of the house for an afternoon, it also gave them a chance at getting some respect in the home that evening. And who can blame them? Many of these elderly immigrants knew very little English. They were thrust into a strange, bustling city where they had only a slippery grasp on the language. Their children and grandchildren were free to leave the home in search of employment, coming back with unfamiliar tales, chattering in an indecipherable tongue. Meanwhile, the matriarchs sat in a corner and watched the slow dissolution of the family they had raised.

"[The story] stirred their minds and memory as with a magic touch, it loosened their tongues and revealed the inner life and thoughts of those who are so often inarticulate. They are accustomed to sit at home and to hear the younger members of the family speak of affairs quite outside their own experience, sometimes in a language they don't understand."

Addams continued, "The story of the Devil Baby, evolved in response to the imperative needs of anxious wives and mothers, recalls the theory that woman first fashioned the fairy story, that combination of wisdom and romance, in an effort to tame her mate and to make him a better father to her children, until such stories finally became a crude creed for domestic conduct, softening the treatment men accorded to women."

> The film *Rosemary's Baby* is based on the story of the Devil Baby of Hull House. Anton LaVey, the founder of the Church of Satan, served as a consultant on the film, and even acted in it.

The immigrant women that flocked to Hull House in that long-ago summer lived harsh lives, even in the middle of the Land of Opportunity. They were plucked from their familiar surroundings, and thrown into the complicated and constantly changing environment of city life. They came to Hull House for help with acquiring food and shelter, but also for something very nearly as basic as those needs: the desire to be heard, the craving for justice and order in this confusing new world. "To them this simple tale with its direct connection between cause and effect, between wrongdoing and punishment, brought soothing and relief, and restored a shaken confidence as to the righteousness of the universe."

The Destination America show *Amish Haunting* featured a tale that is eerily similar to the story of the Hull House Devil Baby. The story is set in Lancaster County, among the Old Order Amish. According to the story, a couple named Ruth and Ezekiel were promised to each other in marriage, but succumbed to temptation and had sex before the wedding. (Again, just as with the Chicago immigrants, a sin in the eyes of the church and of their society leads to tragedy.) Ruth became pregnant. The couple married, and hired a midwife from outside the community to help when Ruth's time came.

The pregnancy was uneventful, but the labor dragged on and on. When the baby was finally born, it was half-human, half-goat – a punishment for the couple's premarital sin. The midwife wanted to smother it, but the parents stopped her. The father took it outside, hoping that the animal cries would be less noticeable if they came from the barn. The mother, Ruth, bonded with the baby, naming it Ezekiel, after its father. (This version, in which the baby is passive and infantile, is different than any version of the Hull House story, in which the devil baby is abusive and mobile, leaping over pews in the church to escape the priest.)

After a few months, Ruth misguidedly brought the goat baby to church, in an effort to introduce him to society. People, predictably, reacted in horror, and Ruth and Ezekiel had to flee, taking baby Ezekiel with them. As the buggy chase ran on, the door of their buggy bounced open, and the goat baby leapt out, running into the fields. Ezekiel kept on driving, realizing that the bishop and rest of the posse would continue to chase their buggy.

Ruth and Ezekiel moved to a Mennonite community, trying to escape the shame of their goat son's birth. On the first anniversary of the birth, still grieving for her missing firstborn, Ruth put a plate of hot food out on the porch in remembrance of the baby's birthday.

According to the show, the Goat Baby is all grown up now, and in the manner of cryptids everywhere, doesn't seem to have aged past adulthood. On winter nights, so the tale goes, families sometimes hear the snarling cries of the Goat Baby prowling around their houses. When this happens, the woman of the house hurries to put a plate of hot food out on the porch, hoping to mollify the creature. Otherwise, the family faces certain ruin as the monster attacks their crops and slaughters their livestock.

The story is told, on the show, by Ruth and Ezekiel's granddaughter. Oddly, she doesn't have the usual Amish reticence about appearing on camera. (As it happens, most of the folks on the show seem perfectly fine with being filmed.) Having a purported family member tell the story is a nice touch, but the tale still smacks of urban legend. A young couple defies the conventions of their society and is punished with demonic retribution? Sounds an awful lot like Chicago in the summer of 1913.

10. POSSESSIONS AND EXORCISM

So, demons are used in advertising. They show up in science, and in folktales, and on the sports field. They are a part of everyday life, all over the world. We in the West fear them, unless they are capering on a football field or on a can of potted meat. Some people in the East see their demons very differently. Sometimes, they have even found a way to coexist with their demons. Muslim women, second-class citizens in a culture that little values them, have even turned demonic possession into a means of personal empowerment.

There are some people that would say that much of what we see as possession is not actually demonic, but rather signs of mental illness. Psychiatrists have been struggling with the difference between the two for many years. How do we know what is mental illness and what is actual possession?

Demonic possession is very real. Very rare, but very real. And true possession is utterly horrifying.

Nick Groff, of the popular television show Ghost Adventures, describes the different levels of demonic torment in his book *Chasing Spirits: The Building of the Ghost Adventures Crew*, written with Jeff Belanger. Nick puts it succinctly:

"People who study demons will tell you there are various types of ways entities can interact with living people, from mild influence to a full-on demonic possession...

"Influence: an entity can influence our lives. It can offer temptations, and can even try to put thoughts into our heads.

"Oppression: [this] means that an entity has targeted a specific person and is not only trying to influence through temptation, but is also putting thoughts into our heads and trying to motivate our actions.

"Attachment: the entity is now staying with us and tempting, oppressing, and even tormenting us. It can cause physical illness – something doctors can't cure – and it can cause depression.

"Possession: [this] happens when the living person turns over control to the entity ...this is the most rare phenomenon."

So how do we know that someone is truly possessed? Let's take, as an example, the story of the Gadarene demoniac. This is the clearest case of possession in the Bible, so we'll use that as our touchstone.

The story of the demon-possessed man in the country of the Gadarenes appears in the Gospels of Matthew (Matthew 8:28-34), Mark (Mark 5:1-20), and Luke (Luke 8:26-39). Jesus, in his wanderings, went to the country of the Gadarenes. He was met by a man who was possessed by demons. The man had a history of appalling behavior; the townspeople would chain him up, but he would break the chains and go wandering off into the wilderness to live among the tombs, screaming, babbling, and cutting himself with sharp rocks. When he saw Jesus, he cried out, "What has the Son of the Most High God to do with me?" Jesus asked the demon residing in the man's body for his name, and the demon replied, "My name is Legion, for we are many." Jesus commanded the demons to come out of the man, and they balked. "Don't send us into the abyss!" There was a herd of pigs grazing nearby, and the demons begged to be allowed to possess the pigs instead. Jesus gave them the go-ahead, and the demons left the man and went into the herd of swine. The possessed pigs threw themselves en masse off of a nearby cliff into the sea, and perished. The swineherds ran to the town and reported all of this. When the people of the town came out to see what was going on, they found the formerly possessed man sitting quietly at Jesus' feet, clothed and completely sane. Instead of being grateful, though, they were terrified, and asked Jesus to leave the area. He did, after telling the recovered man to spread the word about what Jesus had done for him.

This story gives exorcists a pretty clear set of guidelines of what to look for in a suspected case of demonic possession. For a point-by-point illustration, we'll take a look at Mark.

Mark 5:2. The demoniac had an unclean spirit. In other words, he had another being inside him, in addition to his own soul.

Mark 5:3. The possessed showed unusual physical strength. No one could bind him.

Mark 5:4. He suffered fits of rage. While bound, he wrenched his chains apart to escape.

Mark 5:6-7. The fourth sign of demonic possession is a split personality (the original human soul, and the demon or demons). The demoniac approaches Jesus for help, but at the same time, cringes away in fear.

Mark 5:7. The possessed shows resistance, and a revulsion for spiritual things. The demoniac tells Jesus to leave him alone, asking what business the Son of God has with him.

Mark 5:7. The demoniac shows clairvoyant powers. He knows immediately who Jesus is.

Mark 5:9. The Gadarene displays an altered voice. When he speaks, a legion of demons speaks using his mouth.

Mark 5:13. The eighth symptom is occult transference. At Jesus' command, the legion of demons leaves the man and enters into the herd of swine.

Of these symptoms of possessions, the second, third, and fourth characteristics are similar to symptoms of mental illness. The mentally ill can be violent, and sometimes, signs of split personality are part of mental trauma.

But the other five characteristics are not psychiatric conditions. Clairvoyance is not usually a sign of mental illness. Neither is guttural, demonic, growling speech, or speaking in a language the possessed person doesn't know. If these signs are present, a psychiatrist has every right to call for a priest, and a priest can be pretty sure he is dealing with a case of true demonic possession.

The Catholics seem to have borrowed an important part of their exorcism from this story as well. It's a vitally important part of an exorcism to find out the demon's name. The first question the priest asks in the sacrament of baptism is, "What is the child's name?" In the New Testament, Jesus called his apostles by name when he asked them to become his followers. With knowledge of a name comes power, and the ability to command. It may be that the early Church fathers realized this, and took their cue from Jesus when he asked the demon its name. In many accounts of exorcism, the crisis moment of the whole affair comes when the demon, using the mouth of the possessed, grudgingly spits out its name. Then the exorcist can use the name to command the demon to leave. By using the demon's name, the exorcist is calling it into the Light, and its power begins to wane.

So here's the next question: how do we know when a possessed person has been cured? It's not all pea soup and blasts of energy. In fact, when possessed people do retch something up, it's very rarely food at all. There have been reports of people being released from possession pretty soon after eating a big meal, and throwing up large amounts of mucus with no trace of food. But in deliverance, there is a lot of retching, coughing, spitting, drooling, foaming, vomiting – anything to get the demonic presence out of the body.

When demonic spirits are cast out, at least in the Christian religion, they normally leave through the mouth or nose. The Holy Spirit is associated with breath; after Jesus rose from the dead he appeared to his disciples and breathed on them, saying "Receive the Holy Spirit" (John 20:22). When an exorcism is successful, there is often a manifestation through the mouth. This doesn't have to be drool or vomit (thank goodness). Manifestations of deliverance can include crying, screaming, sighing, yawning, or belching. But this doesn't mean the exorcism was a failure. People who sigh out their demons are just as delivered as those who have more violent manifestations.

Another disconcerting aspect of possession is that while possessions happen in real time, demons are timeless. Archbishop Ron Feyl, the Presiding Bishop of the Sacred Order of Saint Michael, points out that one demon, say, one of the heavy hitters like Leviathan, can possess many different people, from a Roman noblewoman in the third century to a milkmaid in 1792 to a banker in 2015 to someone in 2376, *all at the same time*. Demons have incredible power, and are not bound by our human concepts of time.

A person doesn't have to be Catholic to be possessed, or to benefit from an exorcism. Muslims believe that people can be possessed by djinns, spirits that can be either good or bad. To cast out an evil djinn, the exorcist performs a special ceremony during which he reads passages from the Koran over the possessed person. Islam considers the exorcism of djinn to be a noble thing, something that the righteous have been doing throughout Islamic history. According to the Koran, the faithful are obligated to help the oppressed, and that includes those who are troubled by djinn possession.

In the Hindu religion, there are numerous books of ceremonies for casting out evil spirits. These involve reciting the names of the Narasimha and reading from the Bhagavata Purana out loud.

In Judaism, a dybbuk is a wandering soul, not necessarily a demon, which has the ability to attach itself to a living person. Possessive evil spirits are mentioned in the Old Testament – King Saul is possessed, and David exorcises the evil spirit by playing the harp. His exorcism doesn't quite do the trick, though. The Book of I Samuel says that Saul was possessed by an evil spirit from the Lord, and David's harp playing was the only thing that would soothe him. But as David was playing, Saul, who had been sitting idly toying with a spear, got the idea to pin David to the wall with it. David nipped out of the way twice, then escaped, fleeing the palace.

In the rabbinical texts of the first century, exorcisms consisted of burning the ashes of a red heifer and the roots of certain herbs around the victim. Herbal amulets were also suggested, as well as reading from the Psalms, saying incantations in the name of King Solomon, and repeating the Divine Name of God.

Nowadays, a Jewish exorcism is performed in much the same way as a Christian exorcism. The exorcist rebukes the evil spirit and forces it to tell the exorcist its name. With knowledge of the name, the exorcist gains power over the spirit, and can cast it out of the possessed person.

The Kabbalah contains rituals for banishing a dybbuk. The exorcism must be performed by a ba'al shem, a miracle-working rabbi. The dybbuk, as a tortured soul rather than a demon, can either be redeemed through the exorcism, or cast into Hell. A dybbuk usually leaves the victim's body through the little toe, leaving behind a small, bloody hole as proof of its exit. (No vomiting here, which has got to be a relief)

The Testament of Solomon is an apocryphal work that explains how King Solomon was able to build his famous Temple – with the grudging help of several demons. The demons were coerced into helping Solomon by means of a magic ring given to the king, interestingly enough, by the Archangel Michael.

The ring, also known as the Seal of Solomon (after he started using it as a signet ring), is described in both Jewish and Islamic tradition as bearing either a pentagram or a hexagram – the six-pointed star later called the Star of David. The ring enabled Solomon to control demons, including Beelzebul, their prince. With Beelzebul under his thumb, Solomon was able to command the entire race of demons, so he put them to work and had them build his Temple.

Belial is also one of the heavy hitters in the demonic hierarchy. In Jewish lore, Belial was created just after Lucifer. Unlike Lucifer, though, Belial was evil right from the jump, and was one of the first angels to revolt against God. Belial was seen as the personification of lies and evil. Belial is also known, in the Testament of Solomon, as one of the djinn.

The demons responsible for building the Temple proved to be quite useful, using their supernatural strength to set the cornerstone of the building. One of the demons, Ephippas, went to the Red Sea and brought back a column for the Temple. Ephippas came back accompanied by another demon, Amelouith. Amelouith claimed to be the demon who supported the Egyptian magicians in their rivalry against Moses, and who had hardened Pharaoh's heart against the Israelites. Amelouith had been caught with the Egyptian host when the parted waters of the Red Sea returned, drowning Pharaoh's army. The demon had been trapped under the pillar until Ephippas came to get it for the Temple. Working together, the demons lifted the pillar, freeing Amelouith.

When Solomon died, he was standing up, leaning on a stick for support. For a year after that, he remained standing there, stone dead. The djinns, not realizing he was dead, kept on building Jerusalem and following Solomon's final order. One day, Solomon's corpse fell over – ants had eaten through the stick, and the body overbalanced. The djinns finally caught on to the fact that their master was dead, so they skipped town.

The apocryphal Old Testament story of Solomon gives us a tantalizing glimpse into the New Testament. While the demons are working on the Temple, Solomon strikes up a conversation with the demon Ephippas, asking why he is so frustrated. The demon answers that he is worried about the only person that could defeat him – a man born of a virgin, who would be crucified by the Romans egged on by the Jews. (This is, admittedly, not fair to the Jews. The original text was written in Greek, sometime between the 1st and 5th centuries CE. So in spite of this ostensibly being a story told firsthand by one of Judaism's most famous kings, it's fairly obvious that the actual author was a Christian writing roughly a thousand years after the time of Solomon)

The Babylonians also believed in a world filled with evil spirits. There was Pazuzu, the demon of the howling north winds who delighted in destroying crops. Another was Lilitu, a hybrid creature who was part human and part bird. This demon roamed the night, draining people of bodily fluids.

The lion-demon was a hybrid, a bare-chested man with the head and tail of a lion, donkey ears, and bird feet. He holds a dagger upraised in one hand and a mace in the other. Strangely, these menacing figures were seen as benevolent entities, protecting humans against evil demons that caused misfortune and disease.

Babylonian and Assyrian texts are rife with mention of demons and witches. Most of the religious cuneiform tablets that survive contain exorcisms to combat these evil forces. In Mesopotamia, as in other ancient and primitive cultures, sickness was seen as being caused by demons. Priests, with their direct line of communication with the gods, were considered to be the first line of defense against these terrifying creatures who brought illness, confusion, and sometimes even death.

When the Jews were captured by the Babylonians and spent decades in captivity, these demoniacal traditions became part of the Jewish culture. From there it was passed on to early Christian culture. (The practice in modern exorcisms of nailing written prayers to the walls of houses requiring spiritual cleansing goes back to the cuneiform tablets of the Sumerians and Mesopotamians) Centuries later, these demons and witches had a terrible renaissance in the European Middle Ages.

I was raised in the Orthodox faith. We didn't talk a whole lot about the devil in our church, except as the natural counterpart to God. We certainly never discussed exorcisms. But they are out there in the world of Orthodoxy.

The very first experience an Orthodox has of the devil is when she is still an infant. Forty days after birth, a child is baptized. Her parents and godparents stand at the baptismal font with the baby, and renounce the devil and all his works on her behalf.

The 8th century Church Father St. John of Damascus had some interesting observations on the behavior and motivations of demons. Orthodox Christianity teaches that since God created Lucifer, he was formed with "no trace whatsoever" of evil. But he wasn't able to sustain that purity, so he rebelled against God. Satan decided of his own free will to depart from good and become evil. Just as darkness is the absence of light, so is evil the absence of goodness.

Demons, in the Orthodox Church, have no power except what God has granted to them. But when God does concede and lets demons attack humans, demons can change themselves into any form in which they wish to appear. St. John does go into great detail about demons' specific abilities:

"Of the future both the angels of God and the demons are alike ignorant: yet they make predictions. God reveals the future to the angels and commands them to prophecy, and so what they say comes to pass. But the demons also make predictions, sometimes because they see what is happening at a distance, and sometimes merely making guesses: hence much of what they say is false and they should not be believed, even although they do often say what is true."

In the early days of the Church, exorcisms were performed by people who were specially trained to pray to drive out evil from the faithful. Exorcisms were so important in the early church that "exorcist" was its own office. Starting in the fourth century, though, the office of exorcist was taken over by priests. Modern Orthodox theology takes a much broader view of exorcism – covering all the bases. Christ is the original exorcist, since He won the victory over the devil. All priests are exorcists as well, because they follow Christ's example by performing the holy sacraments and preaching the Word of God. The Orthodox Book of Prayers includes three prayers of exorcism by Saint Basil and four by Saint John Chrysostom. These prayers ask in the name of God to deliver the possessed from the captivity of the devil. Saint Benedict lived before the schism between the Orthodox and Catholic Churches, so he is revered in the Orthodox Church as well. (Much more on him later. He made quite a name for himself as an exorcist, and he's earned the title)

And all Orthodox Christians are considered exorcists as they struggle against personal sin and social evil. Archbishop Iakovos, speaking at Cornell University, pointed out that "the whole Church, past, present, and future, has the task of an exorcist to banish sin, evil, injustice, spiritual death, the devil from the life of humanity" (Exorcism and Exorcists in the Greek Orthodox Tradition, March 10, 1974).

There is another way the Orthodox Church fights against the evil powers of Satan. This is a quirky rite called vaskania, designed to avert the evil eye. Vaskania is a particularly Greek idea, a holdover from ancient superstition. Primitive people believed that some people have such powerful feelings of jealousy and envy, that when they looked at some beautiful object or person, they could destroy it simply through this power. Vaskania is recognized by the church as the jealousy of some people for things they don't possess, even intangibles like beauty, courage, youth, or any other blessing. There are prayers to avert the curse and destruction of the evil eye. The church accepts the fact of human jealousy, and these prayers are a silent recognition of this phenomenon as a morbid feeling of envy.

Although the church frowns on the faithful going to seers or fortune-tellers to remove the evil eye, there is a secret rite performed by some people that certainly sniffs of magic. The exorcist (not a priest but an old woman) prepares a vial of olive oil and a small glass of water. She dips a finger into the oil, makes the sign of the Cross with it on the victim's forehead and lets one drop fall into the water. She repeats the process, making a cross on the forehead, on the chin and on both cheeks. If the devil is present, the four drops of oil in the water will join to form the ellipsoid shape of an eye. The ritual then calls for the reading of prayers. Then the exorcist repeats the four signs of the Cross. If the exorcism has been successful, the drops of oil will not join in the water, but will float separately.

As I was working on this book, looking at exorcism in different religions and cultures, I was struck by an odd thought. We know some Christian sects are more invested in exorcism than others. The charismatics and the Pentecostals have a thriving deliverance ministry. The Catholics have practically cornered the market on exorcism, both in the United States and in predominantly Catholic countries like Italy. But you don't hear much about exorcisms in, say, the Lutheran church, or the Episcopalian church. There are churches and communities that are aware of demonic intent, and those that seem ... well, a little less concerned with the whole business. That got me thinking. I thought, you know, you never hear of an Amish exorcism. Hmm.

So on a whim, I sat down at the computer one day and typed "Amish demon" into Google. That led me on an odd little detour down one of the stranger rabbit holes of the Internet. I came across a show on Destination America (a wife-beater t-shirt-wearing poor cousin of the Discovery Channel) called *Amish Hauntings*.

This show caters to our current fascination with anything Amish, and anything paranormal. Smash them together in a blender and hit puree a few times, and this show will ooze out when you lift the lid. Amish folk are shown on camera, sharing tales of horror from their communities. (This isn't quite as odd as it seems at first. Just as with the prohibition against driving cars, but not against riding in them, some Amish are okay with being filmed, as long as they aren't the ones wielding the camera. Even so, there were a few speakers who insisted on having their faces blurred when they did their interviews) Apparently, as the show's intro promises, living the simple life won't protect you from the demonic, the terrifying, or the creepy.

The very first show told the tale of a young Amish girl, Sarah Lapp, who was given a doll by her non-Amish neighbor, as a birthday present. Amish children play with dolls, but the dolls are faceless. Making a doll with a face goes against the religious injunction not to make graven images. The girl, enamored with the doll, ran with it into the house, ignoring the shouts of her mother to stop. Inside the house, her horrified father grabbed the doll and tossed it into the fireplace to burn the offending image. But the damage had been done – Satan had been invited into the house, all because of a doll with a face.

The trouble continued the next day. At Sarah's birthday party, some unseen force blew out the candles on her cake before she could make a wish. The girl became more and more withdrawn over the next few weeks. Sarah's older brother, Jeremiah, declared that Sarah's eyes were filled with hatred as she gazed at her family. Finally, the bishop came to Sarah's parents with a troubling revelation. Sarah's teacher had been looking over her students' shoulders as they worked on their penmanship. In Sarah's penmanship notebook, the young girl had scribbled "Burn in Hell" over and over.

Sarah was removed from her home and sent to prayer camp, as a way to sort of "reboot" her faith. While she was gone, though, demonic activity in the Lapp home ramped up.

Samuel Lapp, Sarah's father, came home one day to find blood spattered liberally all over the walls of the house. Frantic, he searched the home for his family. He found Jeremiah in the barn. The boy was unhurt, but had slaughtered one of the family's pigs and threw blood everywhere. The boy had skinned the pig's face from its skull and was wearing it like a mask.

Samuel pleaded with the bishop to come to his house and help Jeremiah. The bishop rushed to the Lapp house and performed an exorcism – which, in the Amish religion, seems to consist mainly of shouting at the demon to leave. After a few hours of this, the demon left. Soon after that, Sarah was allowed to rejoin her family, and all was well.

The stories on *Amish Haunting* have a common theme: don't screw up. These horror stories result from the barest of infractions. A girl brings a doll with a face into the home, and Satan moves in soon after. An engaged couple has sex before their wedding, and as a result, the wife gives birth to a half-human, half-goat baby. A farmer decides not to bless the seed before he plants, and tragedy soon follows. The takeaway from all of this seems to be to point and whisper about the Amish. See how strict their rules are? You can get yourself in trouble with the demonic for the littlest things!

The question uppermost in my mind was this: how true are these stories? Do they have just a grain of truth to them? Are they made up out of whole cloth for the show? (While trying to find out, I did run across a website in which a paranormal fiction writer said he had pitched some ideas to the show, and was waiting to hear if the producers were going to use them.) The question of whether or not these stories are true is beyond the scope of this book. That being said, there may still be something to be learned from this train wreck. I discussed a couple of the demonic cases with James Tyson, host of *Spaced Out Radio Weekend*. His reaction, without commenting on the veracity of the stories, was simple and elegant. "Manifestation is a powerful thing. It's possible that Amish society walks such a fine line in their religious beliefs that any deviation has horrible consequences. It may be that any infraction of the rules leads to an unconscious manifestation of this horror."

So, whether or not these particular stories are true, or if they are just made up for ratings, doesn't matter. Even if these stories weren't filmed, they would still have resonance for the people who experienced them. If an Amish farmer believed that not blessing his seed corn before planting it would lead to the failure of his crops, that's what would manifest. That could easily result in financial ruin and embarrassment in the community. (In this story, the destitute farmer hanged himself in his barn. A hundred years later, the farmer who bought the property on which the barn stood ran afoul of the suicide's angry ghost)

There's something else to consider too, while watching this show. The area in which the show is set, northern Pennsylvania (more specifically, Lancaster and Chester Counties), is the birthplace of Pennsylvania Dutch hex magic. Around 50 percent of the population in the area claim Pennsylvania Dutch ethnicity. Of those, around 10 percent are Plain People, or Amish and Conservative Mennonites. So these 10 percent could be drawn, by heritage and by culture, to the practice of hex magic ... which is considered sinful by their church. This could create quite a cognitive dissonance for these folks.

In the world of hex magic, the practice is carefully divided into braucherei (white magic) and hexerei (black magic) – that is, if the practitioner isn't Amish. For the Old Order Amish and Conservative Mennonites, it's all black magic. Even the brightly colored hex signs on barns, and the cheerful little distelfink birds, symbols of good luck, are considered sinful abominations.

A big component of hex magic involves herbal medicine. There's absolutely nothing wrong with using natural cures; people have been doing it for centuries, and it works. But even something as simple as making a healing balm out of olive oil, beeswax and comfrey root can have dire spiritual consequences, if the person making it happens to be Old Order Amish. That thought form, that assumption that anything to do with hex magic is evil, can lead to a manifestation of the demonic. Even if these manifestations are purely imaginary, they have an effect on the person experiencing them.

Another interesting snippet is purely geographic. Northern Pennsylvania's soil is very high in limestone, a fact which drew the first settlers there. A soil with a high limestone content is considered more productive, as it holds the moisture better. Limestone is also considered to be an attractant of paranormal phenomena. It's created from the calcified skeletons of tiny water-living organisms. Since it's made from something that was once alive, it's said to hold the power to attract paranormal activity, such as orbs and electronic voice phenomena, or EVPs.

So is *Amish Haunting* even worth watching? I think it is. This is just a personal opinion, of course. But it is interesting to see what a fine line the Amish walk in regards to their religion. Religion is such an integral part of Amish society, that any misstep has consequences not only for one's social standing, but also for one's immortal soul. It's sobering to realize this.

It's interesting to note that early Christianity claimed to have the best track record in successful exorcisms. And it's not surprising. Jesus made a name for himself driving out demons. He had the power of God behind him.

This was not lost on the early Christians. They saw themselves as followers of Jesus, and threw themselves into emulating him, even to the performing of exorcisms. Justin Martyr, writing in the early days of the church, noted that many Christians were having great success at curing demoniacs, even those who had not responded to exorcists of other faiths.

There was actually a reason for this. We know now that there are certain requirements for a successful exorcism; most importantly, the exorcist needs absolute and total faith in the work he or she is about to do, a sense of success no matter what. The early Christians had that in spades. They felt an unshakeable sense of victory due to their faith in Christ. And why not? These were believers whose faith was still fresh, whose religion was still young. They weren't bogged down with two millennia of dusty doctrine and second-guessing. These early exorcists were on fire with their faith. No one had yet said they couldn't cast out demons, so they went ahead and did it.

There are some modern priests who doubt the presence of Satan or demons in the modern world. It's a scary proposition, to believe in demons. It's much easier just to believe in angels and leave it at that. But consider this: the environment in which the gospels were written was at the height of the Roman Empire, one of the most culturally advanced civilizations on the planet. And the Romans borrowed a lot of their cultural chops from the Greeks – again, a civilization renowned for their wisdom. So if we look at the writings of the gospels – a product of their times – and discount everything they have to say about demons, Satan, and the invisible world, that's tantamount to admitting that Jesus was simply some benighted peasant in scratchy robes.

Satan appears all throughout the Bible, in different guises. He is there in the Garden of Eden, as the serpent. He is there at the end, in the book of the Revelation, a symbolic player in the Apocalypse. Whether you see the Bible as the divinely inspired Word of God, or if you simply consider it to be one of the many books written by humans to give other humans a set of guidelines for getting along in life, the fact remains that the Devil, along with God, is one of the main characters.

This is something that marks an evolution in religious thought, setting the Judeo-Christian religions apart from polytheism. However, even polytheistic religions have a certain duality to them. In the cast of dozens of gods and goddesses of the Egyptian pantheon, the ones that stand out are Osiris and Set; good versus evil is the foundation of that ancient culture. The gods of the Greeks and Romans all carry within them the possibility of being benevolent or vicious. Rather like the humans whose lives they oversaw, it just depended on what sort of mood they were in at the time.

It was Judaism and Zoroastrianism, then Christianity, with Islam following soon after, which came up with the idea of one God, and one Satan. This next level, getting rid of a pantheon of gods in favor of just one God, represents an evolution of religious thought. Satan is not considered a god, but maybe he should be, just to keep things in balance.

Imagine someone in medieval Europe who suddenly starts acting abnormally. He can no longer hold down a job, he has fits, he loses the power to communicate effectively with the people around him. Today, we might say he had suffered some sort of nervous breakdown, or was depressed, or that he had otherwise lost touch with reality.

> Some cultures, like the voodoo practitioners of Haiti, don't see possession as being necessarily a bad thing. Worshippers participating in a voodoo ceremony may invite possession by the orishas. They see this as a kind of psychotherapy - a way to integrate parts of their personality that are otherwise suppressed by their roles in society. A man might allow himself to be "ridden" by Erzulie, the goddess of love, in order to get in touch with his feminine side. A mousy woman infused with the powerful spirit of Baron Samedi might discover her inner fierceness after the experience.

Even for us living in the modern age, this is difficult to grasp. This is why mental illness is so terrifying. Here we have a person who doesn't look any different than they did yesterday – but now, we can't understand them. We look into their eyes, and a stranger looks back at us. The lights are on, but nobody's home.

So if someone is out of touch with consensual reality, the logical explanation could be that they are experiencing a different reality. For a medieval person, this hidden reality was the world of demons and spirits. Therefore, in the medieval world, madness equaled demonic possession.

By the time the Age of Reason rolled around, the idea had switched to exactly the opposite. With the coming of the scientific method, showing signs of demonic possession became the hallmarks of madness. Pierre Janet, a psychiatrist and a contemporary of Freud, encountered cases like this in his work at the Salpetriere Hospital in Paris.

A man with a case of suspected possession spent four years in the Salpetriere Hospital.. The hospital was founded in 1656, and still serves patients today – it's where Princess Diana died in 1997. In the first half of the 19th century, the hospital became known for its humanitarian reforms in the treatment of the violently insane. When Dr. Jean-Martin Chacot (1825-1893) took over the psychology department, the Salpetriere became renowned as a center for psychiatric care. Dr. Chacot had a colleague, Dr. Pierre Janet (1859-1947), a psychologist who became a pioneer in the field of traumatic memory. Janet is considered one of the founding fathers of psychology. He coined the words "dissociation" and "subconscious", and was a powerful influence on later psychologists, notably William James, Freud, and Jung. Pierre Janet was also one of the first people to theorize a connection between a patient's past life and present day trauma.

A man in his early thirties, whom Dr. Janet referred to as "Achille" in his writings, came to the Salpetriere in the late 19th century, when Dr. Chacot was in charge of the Psychological Laboratory there. Achille had a normal childhood, including being bullied by his classmates at school. He left school early, started a business, and married young.

Late in the winter of 1890, Achille went on a business trip, which lasted a few weeks. When he returned home, his wife noticed an abrupt change in his personality. He shut himself off emotionally from his wife and his young daughter. At first, he was gloomy and preoccupied, and spoke very little to them. Then, according to Janet's case study, the problem got worse. "His silence assumed a quite peculiar aspect: it ceased to be voluntary as at first; Achille was no longer silent because he did not wish to speak, but because he was not able to speak. He made fruitless efforts to utter a sound and could no longer manage it; he had become dumb."

Achille visited a doctor, who ran him through a battery of tests. The doctor came up with a laundry list of possible ailments – an imbalance of humor, angina, maybe even diabetes – which seems to have given Achille a jolt. He reclaimed his power of speech, using it mainly to "complain of all sorts of pains".

Achille slipped into a black depression. He stopped responding to questions, and seemed to be fading quickly. He kissed his wife and daughter, then lay down on his bed.

He stayed there for two days. "Suddenly, one morning, after two days of apparent death, Achille arose, sat up with both eyes wide open, and broke into a frightful laugh," Janet wrote. "It was a convulsive laugh which shook the whole body, a laugh of unnatural violence which twisted his mouth, a lugubrious laugh which lasted for more than two hours and was truly satanic."

Achille went from the blackest depression to a manic state. He said that demons were cutting and burning him; he reported that he was surrounded by a crowd of capering imps, which were forcing him to say blasphemous things. His arms and legs became grotesquely twisted as he writhed in fits. He escaped his sickroom and fled into the woods, trying to outrun his crippling depression. He wandered into a nearby cemetery and was found several times curled up asleep on a grave, exhausted by the demonic struggle within him. He tried to commit suicide by poisoning himself with laudanum and other strong medications. He even tied his feet together and threw himself into a pond. He managed to claw his way back to shore, though. He dragged himself onto the bank and lay on the grass, weeping with frustration. The test for witchcraft was to throw the suspected witch into the water with her hands and feet bound. If she drowned, she was innocent – but if the water refused her and she floated, she was a witch. Achille saw his survival as a failure of this self-administered test.

After three months of this hell, a doctor suggested to Achille's wife that she should admit him to the Salpetriere, as it was known "as the most propitious place today for the exorcism of the possessed and the expulsion of demons." (Janet)

Dr. Charcot handed the case over to Dr. Janet, who wrote, "I at once remarked in (Achille) all the recognized signs of possession as described in the medieval epidemics." Achille muttered blasphemies constantly under his breath, cursing God and the Virgin Mary. He argued with the demon, using different voices. He still suffered convulsions, his arms and legs twisting with the demonic tortures.

Dr. Janet tried to hypnotize Achille, but he wouldn't go under, and the demons in him mocked the psychologist's efforts to treat his patient. But Janet kept trying. He noticed that Achille, while hallucinating, would make random movements with his hands. He slipped a pencil between Achille's fingers, and the patient gripped it without noticing. Janet then slid a piece of paper under Achille's hand. With a bit of encouragement, Achille started to make absent-minded marks on the paper, even writing his name without realizing it.

Dr. Janet let Achille go on ranting, but stood behind him, and quietly asked him to do certain tasks. Achille ignored him, but the automatic writing continued, and he jotted, "I won't."

Janet interpreted this as coming from the demon inside his patient, so he pressed on. "'And why won't you?' ... The hand replied immediately by writing: 'Because I am stronger than you.' 'Who are you then?' 'I am the devil.' 'Ah, very good, very good! Now we can talk!' It is not everyone who has had the chance of talking to a devil; I had to make the most of it."

Janet appealed to the devil's vanity. "I don't believe in your power, nor shall I do so unless you give me a proof." The devil played right into the doctor's plan, and asked what proof Janet needed. " 'Raise this poor man's left arm without him knowing it.' Immediately Achille's left arm was raised."

The psychologist got Achille's attention, pointing out that his left arm was raised. The patient, confused, put his arm down with some difficulty. Achille grumbled that the demon had played a trick on him. Dr. Janet continued to command the demon, which responded through Achille's body. "He made Achille dance, stick out his tongue, kiss a piece of paper, etc. I even told the devil, while Achille's mind was elsewhere, to show his victim some roses and prick his finger, whereupon Achille exclaimed because he saw before him a beautiful bunch of roses and cried out because he had had his fingers pricked…"

Then, Janet wrote, he went further in his suggestions, and he did "what the exorcists never thought of doing". He asked the devil to make Achille sit in an armchair and go to sleep.

"I had already tried, but in vain, to hypnotize this patient by addressing him directly, and all efforts had been useless; but this time taking advantage of his absence of mind and speaking to the devil, I succeeded very easily … the devil did not know into what a trap I had lured him: poor Achille, whom he had sent to sleep for me, was now in my power. Very gently I induced him to answer me without waking, and I thus learnt a whole series of events unknown to everyone else, which Achille when awake in no way realized, and which threw an entirely new light on his malady."

The story that unfolded while Achille was in a "sleepwalking" state revealed a whole different reason for his troubles. Achille had mixed a little pleasure in with his business trip, and had cheated on his wife. The guilt overwhelmed him, and he started to slip into depression. "He was above all things anxious to hide his misadventures from his wife and this thought drove him to watch his lightest word … it was this which hampered him when he wished to talk."

Achille felt so guilty that he dreamed his own death – and it went so far that he lay motionless for two days solid, as he experienced it and acted it out. During this "death", he naturally was judged, and his subconscious condemned him to Hell for his cheating.

"He dreamt that, his death being an accomplished fact, the devil rose out of the pit and came to take him. The patient … remembered perfectly the precise moment during which this deplorable event took place. It was towards eleven o'clock in the morning, a dog was barking in the courtyard at the time, disturbed no doubt by the stench of hell; flames filled the room, innumerable imps struck the poor wretch with whips and amused themselves by driving nails into his eyes, while through the lacerations in his body Satan took possession of his head and heart."

Dr. Janet, ever the probing psychologist, was fascinated by the way Achille's guilty conscience cooked up elaborate dreams, and how these dreams manifested as apparent demonic possession. Achille cursed and blasphemed, had a demoniacal laugh, heard and saw devils capering around him, and even suffered convulsive torsions of his limbs while gripped in this delirium. "Achille's mouth utters blasphemies, that is the dream itself; but Achille hears them, is indignant, attributes them to a devil lodged within him, this is the action of the normal consciousness and its interpretation. The devil then speaks to Achille and overwhelms him with threats, the patient's interpretation has enhanced the dream and sharpened its outlines…"

Dr. Janet managed to cure Achille, not by performing an exorcism, but by directing his hallucinations. Achille's problem wasn't actual possession, but severely repressed guilt over cheating on his wife. Janet worked with that. "The memory of his transgression was transformed in all sorts of ways thanks to suggested hallucinations. Finally Achille's wife, evoked by a hallucination at the proper moment, came to grant complete pardon to her spouse, who was deserving of pity rather than blame."

Achille made great progress, but traces of his delirium still lingered. After only a few days, he was able to laugh at the idea that he had been possessed, and suggested that maybe he had read too many fairy tales. But he still dreamed of the torments of Hell at night. "The delirium also existed in the subconscious writing where the devil boasted that he would soon reclaim his victim. These facts still show us therefore the last traces of the delirium which might persist without our knowledge."

Thanks to Dr. Janet's psychotherapy, Achille recovered completely from his "possession" experience. Even now, over 125 years later, exorcists must be vigilant when investigating possible cases of possession. Exorcists agree that it's very important to discern whether a victim is suffering from actual possession, or if they are suffering equally from a delusion or some other mental illness. And with good reason – if its mental illness rather than demonic possession, putting the victim through the stress and drama of an exorcism can do more harm than good by reinforcing a delusion of evil.

We know this nowadays because of early psychologists like Dr. Janet. In the late 19th century, doctors were beginning to realize that not all cases of possession were caused by actual demons. Sometimes, what looked like demonic possession was mental in origin, not spiritual.

It takes the gift of discernment to ascertain what is, and what is not, a demonic attack. Part of discernment involves simply asking questions. This helps the exorcist – or the therapist – decide whether they are dealing with a case of demonic oppression or possession, or mental illness. Questions include the gathering of basic information, like religious background; was the patient baptized, or raised Christian? Have they had previous mental health issues, or a history of physical or sexual abuse? Have they suffered from addictions, such as to drugs, alcohol, food, or pornography? Have they had any involvement with the occult? This information gathering is one of the main tools of the trade, whether for a therapist or a priest. We now have a history of psychiatry to help us discover if the affliction stems from a medical, mental, or preternatural source. With the involvement of science, a priest can rule out natural causes before assuming that a problem is supernatural.

Skip Heitzig, at one time the pastor of the charismatic Calvary Chapel of Albuquerque, put out a tape in the 1980s entitled "Demon Possession". This presentation detailed his work in the field, and some of his personal experiences. In the tape, Heitzig cautioned his listeners to keep to the middle of the road when it came to believing in demonic attacks. It's dangerous not to believe in demons, but it's also problematic to believe too much, to see demons under every bed and in every twitch of the limbs. He quoted a Christian psychiatrist's report that the thousands of patients he'd treated who claimed to be demon possessed only demonstrated that demons are quite allergic to thorazine. Give a patient a good dose of thorazine for a week or two, let the voices in their heads quiet down, and the demons were no longer an issue.

"[The patients] felt less guilty when they could convince themselves that their thoughts were coming from external sources such as demons," the psychiatrist said. Sounds an awful lot like Dr. Janet's experience with Achille.

But enough of the unexplained swirls around to keep exorcists busy ... and to keep paranormal investigators on their toes.

11. PERSONAL EXPERIENCES

Wesley Theobald, a paranormal investigator, had an eerie brush with the demonic as a child. "I was about seven years old, and my brother and I were horsing around in the bedroom." The family had moved into the house in Peoria just a few months before, and Wesley and his brother were having a ball exploring the old house. Wesley's attention was captured by some boards nailed up over a hole in the bedroom wall.

"It looked like the previous owner had boarded up a crawlspace. My dad warned me not to take the boards off." But like many young boys, Wesley couldn't resist the lure of exploration.

"I got a crowbar and pried the nails out of the boards, and pulled the boards away from the hole." The nails came free with a screech, and the last board clattered to the floor. Wesley put the crowbar down and peered into the blackness of the crawlspace.

At first, he couldn't see a thing. But as his eyes adjusted, he realized that he was looking at -- something -- a black mass that lurked in the shadows. He heard a low, warning growl...

"I heard what sounded like multiple growls all at once, but coming from the same entity, the same being. Like all in unison at that exact moment, but different pitches and levels and tones."

Wesley grew up to be a seasoned paranormal investigator, and even at the age of seven, he was fearless. He stuck his left hand into the blackness. He felt along the wall for a light switch. Finding nothing, he waved his hand through the air, searching for a pull string.

Pain lanced through his palm, and he jerked his hand back with a yelp. "I don't know if it was a bite or a scratch, but something tagged me good." He looked in disbelief at the blood dripping from a dozen scratches. Something shifted in the darkness. Something large...

Wesley scrambled to his feet and fled screaming from the room. "I had never seen so much blood in my life. I mean, I've fallen and scraped my knee. I've stepped on glass. But this ... this was serious." He ran to his dad, whimpering as he held out his wounded hand.

"I told you not to go sticking your hand in there!" his dad groused as he drove to the emergency room. "There could be anything in that crawlspace. You probably scratched your hand on some broken wood, or a nail sticking out of the wall."

But Wesley knows better. He knows he saw a black, formless shape skulking in the shadows. It took eighteen stitches to close the scratches -- or bites -- on his hand. It's not lost on him that eighteen can be divided into six ... and six ... and six.

Wesley still has scars on his left arm. They are faint reminders of that day, faded with the passing of years.

That was Wesley's very first encounter with the paranormal. From then on, he was hooked. "That's what made me want to investigate the unknown. It was amazing. I mean, it wasn't amazing that my arm got shredded!" he laughs.

Wesley has also had a brief encounter with demonic possession. He was exploring the basement of the Bowen Building at the Peoria State Hospital with some friends. After the asylum closed in 1973, vandals broke into the highly visible Bowen Building. It has long been rumored that misguided people tried to perform summoning rituals in the basement of the building. Some people feel that those rituals succeeded.

As the group was leaving the basement, Wesley had a strange experience. "I felt warm for a tiny second. Then I felt frigidly cold, like I'd stepped into a meat freezer. I suddenly heard a million voices in my head, people whispering, talking, asking me questions. I couldn't answer them – I couldn't control myself. I felt trapped in my own mind. I could see what was going on, but something was speaking for me, using my own voice.

"It was during this time that I could read people's thoughts, and see them as they actually were. It was as if whatever had possessed me allowed me to hear them and see into their minds, see how they felt about other people, about me. Was that scary?

Hell yes it was." (This fits with demonic lore. Many accounts of exorcism speak of the possessed having preternatural knowledge of the thoughts of others. During the rite of exorcism, a demon will often rail at the exorcists, spilling secret sins. Remember, these demons have had eternity to study humans)

Wesley was possessed for a week. For the first three days, he hid in his home, refusing to speak to anyone. His friends tried to help, but he pushed them away.

"They told me I'd changed. I was mean, nasty, rude towards people. I'd cuss them out, I'd flip them off, I'd tell them to fuck off. That's not me."

Wesley's friends later told him that about three days into his ordeal, he started lightening up a little. He was still rude, but not as nasty as he'd been when they first left the building.

"When the possession was getting near the end, it was like a dimmer switch was being turned down. For a few days, things just got darker and darker, until they went completely black. Then I opened my eyes.

"I think that darkness was the demon trying to overpower me, but it wasn't winning. When I opened my eyes, I felt a lot better. I felt like I could breathe again."

"So it was like your own psyche was fighting off the demon, like your body would fight off a cold?" I suggested.

"Right," Wesley said. "I felt so much better. I called up all my friends and said, come to my house, something amazing just happened."

Wesley still isn't sure that what possessed him for a week was truly evil. "There are so many demons out there, of sorrow, depression, hatred, malice, anger ... I felt those. I was not happy once during that week."

Wesley's experiences have left him eager to do more exploration of the unknown. "Having those encounters with the other side – twice – just made me more intrigued. That's why I continue looking for the unknown. I will not stop until I die."

"Demons are demons. They have never been human. They're an entirely different creature altogether." David Youngquist is another paranormal investigator who has had an encounter with evil. He points out that 95% of the time, anything nasty an investigator will run into is a human soul. "But humans being what they are, you've got the good, the bad, and the ugly." Just because an investigator is dealing with an obnoxious spirit doesn't mean that spirit is demonic.

As we've seen, though, Eastern culture is more fluid in its concept of "demon" than Western culture is. A few years ago, David told me a fascinating story that illustrates the difference between demons and really foul spirits. In this story, an evil spirit was causing serious problems for the living. I've chosen to include this story to illustrate the nasty attitude of this particular spirit – an attitude that bordered on demonic.

One of David's ghost-hunting friends was a young Cambodian man named Thuy. He, his aunt, two siblings, and his grandmother were the only members of their family to escape the slaughter of their village by the Communists. Thuy was away from the village at the time of the massacre. As he was coming home, he heard gunfire. He slipped into the village, avoiding the Khmer Rouge soldiers by coming in a back way. He found his relatives, and they all snuck out the way he had come in. Out of the population of the village, only the five of them survived.

Years later, Thuy met David and another investigator, Kelly Meagher. As they became friends, Thuy opened up to David and Kelly about some of the problems he'd been having. He felt like he and his family were under some sort of supernatural attack. He and his partner had been scratched and pulled out of bed. He showed David the scratches on his arm, and mentioned the scratches on his back. "They looked like cat scratches – they were pretty deep – but he said they didn't have a cat."

Other members of Thuy's family had also suffered attacks from invisible beings. The attacks were never consistent, nor did they follow a pattern. Different family members were targeted at different times.

Kelly and David are both sensitive to the paranormal. As they sat and talked to Thuy, they both picked up on the fact that something had followed him to the meeting that evening. That's when they heard the story of Thuy's escape from his home village.

"The entity wasn't fond of either one of us because it realized we could pick up on it," David told me. The meeting broke up, and everyone went their separate ways.

"Kelly will hear an entity before she sees it. It just depends on whether or not they want to reveal themselves to her. Sometimes, I'm able to hear them and see them. I hear the voices – so does she – but I have to have the time and the energy to completely focus on the spirit in order to see them."

This particular spirit decided that since David could see it, it would have to scare him away. So it went on the attack. "She would show up at work. She couldn't do much in the way of harm, but she could annoy me and distract me. It's a very distracting thing, when you're trying to carry on a conversation, to have an entity like that prowling around.

"I finally got fed up with her one day. She showed up while I was driving home from work one day, and started threatening not only me, but my family too. I just said, 'You know, I've had enough of your crap.' I reached over to the passenger seat of the F-150 I was driving and I grabbed her. I don't think she thought I could do that. I didn't think I could do it either! But it was one of those weird things where I just thought, I gotta do *something*. I just focused my will, I guess."

David was driving past a cemetery at the time. He drove into the cemetery and parked in front of a mausoleum that was built into the side of a hill. Still holding the struggling spirit, David got out of the truck.

"I said, 'I've had enough of your crap – you're gonna stay here for a while. I don't know what I had ahold of her by, but she couldn't get away from me. I walked her down the hill to the vault, and I stuffed her in. Then I said a prayer and sealed her in there. I was wearing a silver cross on a chain around my neck. I took it off and threaded the chain through the mausoleum doors. She definitely didn't like that, when she tried to get out and found that she couldn't.

"I left her there for a couple of days. Every day I'd go back to check on her. When I got close to the vault, I could feel her presence, and she'd get kinda threatening. On the third visit, though, she was just curled up in a ball in the corner of the mausoleum.

"When I saw this entity, she was dressed in a military uniform, and she wore this bright red scarf covering half of her face. I could only see one eye. When she finally calmed down, I talked to her, trying to find out what was going on, and why she was bothering Thuy.

"She told me her name was Ming Na, and she blamed Thuy's family for her death. She turned to me and unwrapped the scarf. She'd been executed – half of her face was blown off.

"She re-wrapped her face and told me that she'd been a Khmer Rouge soldier. Her superior needed someone to blame for Thuy's family's escape, and he'd blamed her. He executed her in the same rice paddy that was the killing field for the rest of the villagers. He marched her out to the edge of the paddy, made her kneel, put an AK47 to the back of her head, and pulled the trigger."

In Asian culture, there are various levels of good and evil. If a person dies with a lot of anger and hatred in their soul, they can acquire enough energy to become a vengeance spirit. They have a stronger ability to affect people and things in our world, which can make them seem demonic. In the case of the spirit David was dealing with, she had been blamed by the leaders of the Khmer Rouge for Thuy's family's escape from the village she was supposed to cleanse. Ming Na was a vain woman, and proud of her looks. Of course she blamed the family for what had happened to her. After her death, her spirit acted in a way we would consider demonic.

"In Asian culture, a vengeance spirit is seen as really bad ass. People will go out of their way to avoid pissing off these spirits. And here I am, grabbing one and stuffing it into a mausoleum!"

Luckily, David has a friend, a woman named Jackie Garner, who is very gifted at helping lost spirits cross over to the Other Side. David called Jackie in California and explained his predicament. After asking, "How the *hell* did you get involved with that?" Jackie asked if Ming Na was still a threat. David said she hadn't been belligerent the last couple of times he'd checked on her. At that point, the spirit had been cooped up for a couple of weeks, and was definitely not happy about it.

Jackie suggested leaving the spirit an offering of food, traditional in Asian culture. So the next time David went to the mausoleum, he left a cupcake from his lunch on the stone steps. He hoped the offering would lead to a rational dialogue with the vengeance spirit.

The gift worked. The next time David spoke with Ming Na, she was calm, and ready to discuss her situation. David asked if she was ready to go to the Other Side, and she admitted that she was afraid to cross over. She said she'd done so much evil in her life that she was scared of the consequences. It took a while, but David finally did talk her into going toward the Light.

"As she went upward to the Light, first her uniform fell away, then the scarf dropped off her face. She went into the Light, and Thuy and his family weren't bothered again."

When the spirit was safely gone, David unwrapped the chain he had threaded through the bars of the mausoleum doors and reclaimed his cross. The chain, once a gleaming silver, was now tarnished a dull, mottled gray.

Troy Taylor has written well over a hundred books on the paranormal. His books blend history and the supernatural in an exciting froth of entertainment and education. He is well known as an expert on many aspects of the paranormal, and is in high demand for radio and television shows. October is a particularly busy time for him.

Dave Glover, a radio host based in St. Louis, called Troy up a few years ago with an exciting proposition. "We've got a show planned for Halloween, and we'd really like you to be a part of it," Dave said, his voice humming with excitement. "I know you're up in Chicago now, but I really hope you can make it down for the show."

Troy had been a regular guest on Dave's show, and one of his most popular subjects was the St. Louis exorcism case. In January of 1949, a young boy, living with his family in Maryland, began showing signs of possession. The boy, referred to by the pseudonym Robbie Doe, experienced the terrifying phenomena of being thrown from his bed, and suffered scratches on his body. The scratches eventually spelled out "Louis", and his family, desperately seeking help, moved across the country to St. Louis, Missouri. In March and April 1949, Robbie came under the care of several Jesuit priests, who prayed over him nightly for much of those two months. (Troy goes into detail about the case in his book *The Devil Came to St. Louis*.) The case formed the basis for William Peter Blatty's book *The Exorcist*, as well as the movie of the same name.

"We're doing the Halloween show on the Exorcist house – actually broadcasting from the house. Can you join us?"

"Honestly, I just wanted to see it," Troy told me. "Sure, I'd had some weird experiences while I was working on the first edition of the book. But to me, it was just a historically cool spot. It was a place I'd been researching for years and years, and I really wanted to see the inside of it."

Troy met Dave, the show's host, and Tom, the producer, out at the house one October evening. Troy and Tom stood around outside catching up for a few minutes, then Dave wandered up.

"Have you been inside yet?"

"No, I just got here," Troy replied. The men walked to the front door of the house. The owner had given the radio show permission to use the house for the night. Dave opened the door and motioned Troy in. "Let's go upstairs."

Troy was familiar with the layout of the house from his years of research on the case. He followed Dave up the stairs, which creaked slightly under their weight.

"Here it is," Dave said as he turned a doorknob and pushed. His voice was hushed, almost reverent. "This is the bedroom where the exorcism took place."

The room was empty – stripped down to the floorboards. The owner had plans to remodel the bedroom, and restore it to the way it looked in that spring of 1949. Dave walked into the room and stood there, turning in a slow circle, drinking in the atmosphere. "Can you believe it? This is where it all happened, right here, right where we're standing."

"I got to the doorway," Troy told me, "and I just froze. I'm not sensitive at all, but I could not walk across that threshold. I just could not walk in. I was just standing there, listening to Dave talk." Finally, Dave looked back over his shoulder at Troy. "So are you coming in or what?"

"I can't. I can't make myself go in."

Dave finally came over and took Troy by the arm, pulling him into the room. "Immediately I was covered in goosebumps. The hair on my arms was standing straight up. It felt like being shocked with a cattle prod. And I hadn't come into it thinking, oh, this is gonna be weird. I didn't head into the evening looking for the ghoulish. I just went into the house thinking, I just want to see this room. There's nothing here, there's no reason for any dark energy to be hanging around. But after everything that happened that night ... I really think there's some sort of lingering presence in that room."

Troy and Dave left the room and headed downstairs to greet the guests for that night's show. The radio station had held a contest, and three lucky winners had been chosen. The winners, a man and two women, were driven blindfolded in a windowless van to the house. They had no idea where they were headed that dark October night. When they got to the house, Dave and Tom sat the three down in the living room, took off their blindfolds, and turned on the television – which had the movie *The Exorcist* cued up to the exorcism scene.

"Maybe you've figured this out by now," Dave told the three, "but you're in the house where that exorcism – the case that inspired this movie – took place in 1949. This is where you're going to be spending the night."

"Oh no I'm not." One of the girls promptly got up from her chair, threw her blindfold to the floor, and walked out the front door. That left two.

"The guy went first," Troy says. "He lasted ten minutes in the room. He kept saying he could hear something moving. Now, the house was completely empty. He was wired up with a mike. So was the girl. We could hear them, but we were in the detached garage at the back of the house. When the guy was in there, we could hear everything.

"He kept saying, 'There's something moving in here ... there's somebody in this room.' He kept on saying that. Then abruptly, he said, 'You know what? I'm done.' And then he left. Ten minutes, that was it."

The girl, meanwhile, was kept outside in the windowless van, secluded from anything that was happening in the house.

"So the guy left, and came into the garage with us, and the producers put the girl into the room. We could hear everything over the speakers in the garage. She made it, seriously, a minute and a half.

"She was sitting in there, and we could hear, over the speakers, something sliding across the floor. She's saying the Lord's Prayer. Then she starts screaming, bloodcurdling screams. Tom was in the garage, and Dave was at the front of the house, outside. They both ran inside to get the girl, to turn on some lights and get her out. She was a total wreck.

"Ever since then, with the feelings I had in that room, and the reactions of those two kids ... I really think there's something in that house."

Troy did hours upon hours of taping for a show about the St. Louis Exorcism for the Discovery Channel. "They kept trying to get me to say on camera that these events were genuine. I kept saying, 'I don't know.' I've been researching this case for over fifteen years, and I still don't know if it's genuine or not.

"I had interviewed Fr. Walter Halloran, who was a Jesuit in training in 1949. He was brought in by the priests to hold this kid down, because he was fighting and thrashing so much. This was at the St. Louis house. Even Fr. Halloran said, 'I don't know. I saw some weird things. I will say I saw the bed levitate off the floor about six inches, but that's the only thing I saw that I couldn't explain.' That was what I had to go by. He was there; I wasn't.

"I listened to all these things. I even talked to the kid who was possessed – well, he's not a kid any more, he's in his seventies – and he said he didn't remember much of it.

"So when the producers of the Discovery Channel show tried to pin me down, I just kept saying, I don't know what really happened. I do know that *something* happened. Something happened to this family that was so earth-shattering that they picked up and moved halfway across the country – in 1949 – on the off-chance that they could find help. That says something to me.

"One of the last interviews I did was in Milwaukee, with an Alexian brother, one of the monks at the hospital in St. Louis where the exorcism ended. I went to the Alexian brothers' retirement home to interview Brother Greg, who had never told his story before. He had cancer, and he was dying. He felt that enough time had passed that he could tell his story.

"This guy sat across from me in his apartment and told me everything he remembered. We talked for about an hour and a half. He was in his early nineties, and very frail. When he started to fade, I made him stop ... but he told me the things he saw, and it was unlike anything else I'd heard.

"He swore that he was there, trying to hold this young boy down, and the boy was levitating a foot off the bed. They all saw it. Things were flying around the room ... we were talking on camera, and some of the things he told me never made it onto the show, I guess because the crew wouldn't even put it in – it was too much for them.

"He was one of the boy's handlers. One day he took the boy out for a walk, and he saw a black cat appear out of nowhere. Fr. Greg was sure that this was another form of the demon that was possessing the boy. He was sure the boy was possessed, and he was *there*. I even asked him – are you *sure* about what you saw? He said, I'm positive, and added, 'Why would I lie to you at this point? There is no doubt in my mind that that boy was possessed. I was there at the beginning, I was there at the end. He was not the same boy.'

"I had to rethink some things," Troy admits. "There are still some things I'm up in the air about. But I have to take Brother Greg at his word. I mean, he was there, and he *swore* to me what he saw. I asked him a hundred different ways, but he stuck to his story. He's a man of God, a retired priest. I have to take him seriously.

"Here was a guy who had devoted his entire life, ninety-plus years, to service to other people, to the mentally ill, to God. Why would he lie to me? What possible reason would he have to lie?"

These investigators had brushes with the demonic. These encounters were terrifying, yes, but brief. The demonic presence Wesley blundered into simply lashed out as a warning to the boy. David was able to bind the malevolent Ming-Na, and shut her up in a mausoleum while he figured out a way to help her move on. And Troy may have sensed a residue of evil in the bedroom of the house that saw inexplicable events.

But what happens when a demonic entity moves into your home, creeps into your life? What happens when evil invades your mind, whispering inside your head?

What do you do when the evil moves in with you?

PART TWO
FERAL TRINITY
A GHOST HUNTER'S ENCOUNTER WITH EVIL

12. LINDA

Summer in central Illinois is hot, sticky, muggy. The combination of summer heat and high humidity can be miserable.

Luckily for people in this area, the Illinois River runs right through the middle of Peoria. The river is a vital part of the community and the surrounding towns. Pekin's Court Street actually dead-ends into the river, turning into a parking lot that slopes gently into the water – the perfect place to launch a johnboat. And for those folks who don't own a boat, the river itself is their playground.

Linda K. was fourteen years old on that summer day, years past. A coltish teenager, she weighed just 103 pounds, and practically lived in her bikini that summer. One particularly beastly day, she and her friends decided to cool off with a dip in the river.

Linda's mother had gone to Tennessee to see her own mother. She had given strict instructions to the teen – Linda was forbidden to go to the river with her friends while her mom was out of town. But the teen had a rebellious streak. Nothing, not words of wisdom from her well-meaning mother, not even the threat of being grounded, was going to keep her from splashing and playing in the cool water of the Illinois River that hot summer day.

Linda was in her bedroom undressing when she heard the voice. *Put on your black one-piece.* Linda frowned, and reached for her bikini. As her fingers touched the silky material, she hesitated. Then, impulsively, she pulled on the black swimsuit instead. She tossed a shirt and shorts over the suit, and ran out to join her friends.

The Illinois River is the heart of Peoria, not only for its beauty, but also for its usefulness. Barge traffic on the river has carved a deep channel in the middle, a channel that the Army Corps of Engineers keeps open with periodic dredging. This channel gives the river a particularly swift current. And it was this current that sucked Linda under at the Cedar Street Bridge in Peoria.

Linda was pushed to the bottom of the river by the force of the water rushing past her. A fish bumped her thigh, then hurried on with a flick of its tail. Linda reached out blindly, disoriented from the tumbling of the water. She grabbed for something to hold onto, but her fingers just sank into the mud at the river's bottom.

The cool water embraced her as the current held her down. Exhausted from her brief struggle, Linda came close to giving up. *I'm just going to go to sleep,* she remembers thinking as the dark water surrounded her.

Her friends weren't about to give up so easily. One boy dived under the surface repeatedly, searching for his friend. The barges that run the river also keep the muddy river bottom churned up with a constant screen of silt, so visibility in the water is usually about an inch and a half – or the distance between your eyes and the glass of your diving mask.

The boy groped blindly, desperately seeking any sign of his friend. His fingers closed around a handful of sodden fabric, and he heaved Linda out of the current and up to the surface.

Clutched in his hand was a fistful of the one-piece bathing suit. He had grabbed the wide back of the suit and hauled Linda to safety.

The voice that saved Linda's life that hot summer day was not an isolated occurrence. She grew up in a family that took the world of spirits as a regular part of daily life. Her mother and grandmother both saw ghosts, and both women paid attention to the clock on the wall that would inexplicably play music in advance warning of the strange. "It was just a regular old wall clock, not a cuckoo clock or anything like that. There was nothing special about it. But it would play music, before any ghostly visitation."

That wasn't the only timepiece that seemed to have otherworldly talents. "We had this cheap little alarm clock, something we got ages ago at Walmart or some other store, just an inexpensive thing that plugged into the wall. Two weeks before my husband's mother died, it started flashing 3:58 … 3:58 … 3:58. And that was the exact time she died. When his dad died, again, two weeks before his dad passed, it started flashing again. 5:17 … 5:17 … 5:17.

"When our youngest grandson was born, that cheap little clock started flashing again. 2:10 … 2:10 … 2:10, for about a month. We went to the hospital for the birth, and I happened to look up at a clock on the wall there. The time read two o'clock. I looked at Jerry and said, 'Oh, Jerry … you don't think…?' So when the proud daddy came out to see us at about 2:15, Jerry's first question was 'When was Truman born?' And Bobby said, 'He was born at 2:10.'

"Jerry went home and threw that clock away!"

Linda is no stranger to the world of the mysterious. "I grew up with spirituality. It was perfectly normal to me. My mom saw her father as a spirit. My grandmother saw her mom. Weird things would happen at my grandma's house. The pages of the Bible would flip, as though someone was standing at the table idly flipping the corner of the Book with their thumb over and over. But there was no one there. My grandma would say, 'Shh-shh...' and point to the Bible ... the corners of the pages would just flip with this soft little rustling sound."

Linda's grandmother also taught the young girl a valuable lesson about interacting with the paranormal. "She told me when I was a child, 'If you're ever in bed, and you see a ghost in the room, don't get up. As soon as your feet hit the floor, that spirit's going to disappear.' She said, 'Ask them – what in the Name of the Father, the Son, and the Holy Spirit do you want? And they will tell you what they came for.' I only got to see my grandmother about four times in my entire life. She lived in Tennessee, and we lived here. My mom didn't own a car, because we were very poor growing up. But I do remember all the things she told me about stuff like that."

Other women in Linda's family have had their share of brushes with the supernatural. The night before Linda's uncle died in Bryceville, Tennessee, Linda's aunt heard a strange thump in the corner of her bedroom.

"That was way back in the day, when people were still 'laid out' in the parlor of the house for the wake and the viewing of the body. The next day, her husband Willie went to the mine, and he died. When they brought his body into the house for the wake, they dropped the casket – and it made a thump that sounded just like the noise my aunt had heard the night before her husband's death."

Linda's mother even came to her after death. One evening, Linda was suffering from a vicious migraine. She was lying in bed, hugging a pillow in agony, resting her pounding head on the pillow.

"I saw my mom. I was wide awake, because I couldn't sleep, not with that pain. I was crying, 'Oh God, I'm going to die, it hurts so bad ...' My mom was standing there. She smiled, and sort of nodded at me, but she was lifting her head instead of dipping it. I said, 'What, Mom? What are you trying to tell me?' She did that funny backwards nod again. Suddenly I understood. 'Are you trying to tell me to lift my head up?' I asked. She did it one more time. I lifted my head up, and the headache went away immediately. She vanished, and I never saw my mom's ghost again."

There were many strange and wonderful things that happened to Linda throughout her childhood. But the greatest gift, she says, was when she came to know the Lord. It happened when she was nine years old, and went with her family to hear an evangelist preach at a revival meeting.

"I don't remember the evangelist's name that came to our little church, a place called Golden Acres Church of the Nazarene. We went there all while I was growing up, but when I was nine years old, I heard a little voice during the service. When the minister gave the altar call, I heard a little voice that said 'Go forward – go pray.'

"I talked back to the voice – I said, 'No, I don't want to.' I was a kid! But the voice said it again. 'You need to go pray.' Again, I said, 'No, I don't want to.' Finally I crawled underneath the pew, trying to escape that little voice. The minister – and my mom – both leaned down to see where I'd gone. The minister kindly said, 'Honey, is God talking to you?' and I whimpered 'Yes!'

"He said, 'What is He saying?' I sniffled, 'He's telling me to go up and pray, but I don't want to. I will tomorrow," I added hastily.

"He said, 'Well, if God's telling you to go now, you really do need to go pray.'

"I remember this so clearly: I don't know what a nine year old would have had on her shoulders, but there's so much of my childhood I don't remember. I went up to the altar, and some people laid their hands on me, and other people laid hands on *them*, and I was covered in people praying for me. And when I got through praying, I felt ten thousand pounds lighter. I just felt like such a weight had been lifted from my shoulders. Whatever a nine year old girl could have been going through at that time, I felt like God had suddenly taken it all from me."

Linda knows, deep down in her heart, that this obedience has saved her several times. She knows that the God she put her trust in so long ago still watches over her.

Linda used to work at Ripper and Associates, in an office building in Peoria. As the office manager, she was often left in the building by herself. She would lock the door for safety, and go about her business.

"Part of my job, of course, was to answer the phone. I never, ever wore a headset to answer the phone. Never. But for some reason, that day, I put a headset on. So this guy knocked on the door. I answered it, and he asked to use the restroom. He said, 'Can I use the restroom please?', and then he just strong-armed his way through the door. He went right past my desk to the restroom, so obviously he had been in the building before.

"I had this feeling in the pit of my stomach that something wasn't right, so I dialed 911 while he was in the bathroom. I told them were I was, and that I was in an office building by myself. I was whispering into the headset that a man had just come in that I wasn't comfortable with at all, and could they please send a car over?

"Just then, the guy came out of the bathroom and came to stand in front of my desk. It was really weird, because I was talking to him in front of me, and to the 911 dispatcher on my headset, at the same time. Thanks to the headset, the guy didn't realize I was on the phone with the cops.

"He said, 'Do I know you?' At the same time, the policeman said in my ear, 'Have you seen him before?' I said, "No, I have never seen you before.' He said, 'Are you sure I don't know you from somewhere?' at the same time the cop said, 'You haven't seen him lurking around there in the past few days?' I answered them both – 'I am really sure I've never see you before.' The guy said one more time, 'That's weird. I really feel like I know you,' just as the cop asked for the third time, 'You're absolutely certain you've never seen him around the building?' I looked this man straight in the eyes, and I said very clearly, 'I'm sorry, but I do not know you at all. I have never seen you or met you before.' It was very strange talking to two people, and answering them both at once.

"The guy said, 'Well, I would like to shake your hand.' I hesitated. I didn't want anything to do with this man, and I sure didn't want to touch him. The cop in my ear said, 'We're almost there. Keep him there for just a little longer. Pacify him – shake his hand.' So I reached over the desk and I took his hand. It felt like I had just stuck my hand into a pit of slime. You know that goop kids like to play with, that snotty green stuff? That's what it felt like when I shook his hand. I've never felt that before, or ever again. It felt just like sinking my hand into a glove full of cold slime. I wanted to run away and wash my hands, but I forced myself to stand my ground.

"In my ear, I heard the cop say, 'Okay, we're here.' The police car pulled up in front of the building and turned on its lights. The guy dropped my hand and immediately rushed out of the building. When I looked out the window, he was getting into a car with two other men in it.

"As soon as he left, I ran to the bathroom and washed my hands over and over. Then I sat back down at my desk, and I prayed, Lord, thank you for protecting me. On any other day, I wouldn't have had that headset on, and I wouldn't have been able to call for help without the man knowing it. One more time, I changed my routine, for no reason that I could explain. I did something I wouldn't normally have done – and it ended up saving me."

Linda has also experienced the supernatural in other ways. When she was a young mother, she had a minor but annoying physical issue. Her hands would ache terribly in cold weather. The winter her youngest son was six years old was a particularly bad one, with wind chills as low as 75 degrees below zero.

Linda's niece heard that a faith healer would be visiting the area. She cajoled Linda into coming with her to the church. At first Linda balked. She wasn't about to go out into the cold, not with the wind chills as bad as they were. But her niece insisted. "Oh, come on. I have a feeling about this," she said.

So Linda went. The two women sat through the service, praying and singing along with the rest of the congregation. Near the end of the service, the healer looked out over the gathered crowd and said something that sent chills down Linda's spine.

"There is someone in this church whose hands are hurting them so bad. God said, lift your hands to the sky and you shall be healed. Receive your healing."

"I turned to my niece and said, 'Hey, that's me!' and I lifted my hands."

When Linda got home, she slid her gloves off and noticed something encouraging. "My hands weren't aching. They were fine for the rest of the evening. I got up the next morning – and my hands were on *fire*. They were on fire from the time I got up until eight o'clock that night ... and then it stopped.

"That day, I called my friend Marian and explained what was going on. I told her about what the healer had said, and that I'd lifted my hands for healing. I said, 'My gosh, Marian, I went to church last night, and my hands are on fire – they are on *fire!*' And she started laughing.

"'Linda, haven't you ever heard of the healing heat of the Lord?'

"'No!' I yelped.

"She was still laughing at me, but fondly. 'It's just like you to think that something's wrong while God is healing you,' she said."

Linda's children have also inherited the family gift of supernatural awareness, although it does make them uncomfortable. "I had a weird dream last night," they'll admit ... but they prefer not to talk about it.

But the rest of Linda's family, and Linda herself, accept it. They accept the dreams that come true, the hunches, the visions. They are gifts from God, completely natural, and Linda takes the gifts graciously.

"I was never afraid. That's what made me such a good investigator. What was scary to other people – hearing voices, seeing spirits – that was just natural to me."

Like so many others who have grown up in environments accepting of the spirit world, Linda became a paranormal investigator. In 2009, she founded the group Central Illinois Ghost Hunters, which quickly became one of the best-known investigative groups in the area. Linda's work building up the group paid off. A few short years after its founding, CIGH had a reputation for caring and professional conduct that brought its members great respect in the field. People called from as far away as Canada to get Linda's advice on missing person's cases.

Such was the group's reputation that CIGH was one of the first ghost hunting groups to investigate inside the Culver House in Decatur, Illinois. Built, according to local legend and records, directly over the site of a Native American burial ground, the house has a long and colorful history. (All of Decatur is like this. In the early days of Decatur's history, there were no really firm laws about where to bury people. So the entire city is rife with ghost stories)

Construction was started in 1881, but not much was accomplished over the next twenty years. The local Indians begged the first owner, Josiah Clokey, not to build a house on their sacred land. Clokey built anyway – then quit in the middle of construction. No one knows why. In 1901, the house was bought by John Culver, who completed the house and turned it into a Victorian gem, one of the true showplaces of Decatur.

Culver was a stonemason – he and his brother James rebuilt Lincoln's Tomb in Oak Ridge Cemetery in Springfield. A photograph of Culver shows a solid, honest-looking fellow, sporting a derby hat and a neatly trimmed mustache. He is sitting on the steps of the house, next to his wife Florence, a pretty, middle-aged woman whose dark cape and beribboned straw hat make her look much more fashion-conscious than her working-class husband.

This couple and their family would soon experience the weirdness that began to plague the mansion. One evening, the Culvers were sitting at dinner when a dark "something" flew down the chimney and into the dining room. Whatever this was, it scared the Culvers so badly that John ordered his workmen to brick up the fireplace – not "board up", *brick* up. The family never used it again.

The Culvers remained in the house until 1943, the year John Culver died. The mansion was unoccupied for the next seven years – but it didn't stand empty. Neighbors reported lights in the windows, and a man's face was often seen peering out of the windows of the library: John Culver's favorite room. In 1950, the house was sold and divided into apartments. The tragic history of the house continued to unfold. There were two suicides in the apartments, in 1958 and in 1966. In May 1979, a fire on the third floor caused more than $90,000 in damage to the once-grand old house. In 1988, a tenant was brutally murdered by her boyfriend. One year after that, according to author Troy Taylor, the house was declared unfit for habitation and was boarded up.

When Central Illinois Ghost Hunters investigated the Culver House, they experienced their share of weirdness. Despite no one being allowed on the third floor because of fire damage, the group heard heavy footsteps above them -- on the third floor. "It was like something was very angry, or wanted us to think it was angry. These were heavy, pounding footsteps, but there was no one up there." In the basement, they felt something very dark – but also experienced something intriguing.

Linda was holding her digital voice recorder, taping the session as the group talked with the spirits. She had stuck her recorder-holding hand through a hole in the basement wall, and announced, "Okay, if you'd like to talk to us, this is your chance."

A voice showed up later on the recorder. *No one has ever talked to me,* it said in a plaintive whisper.

Even with that hopeful little voice showing up on the recorder, there's no escaping the fact that the Culver House is brimming with bad vibes. "People will cross the street to avoid walking past that house," Linda says. "There's still something very dark there. Maybe it's trapped, maybe it's there by choice. But it's *there,* and people are reacting to it, even if they don't know it."

Spirits seem to recognize that Linda is special. The very first investigation that Central Illinois Ghost Hunters went on was to a cemetery outside of Bath, Illinois. As soon as Linda walked through the gates, the recorders picked up excited, dismayed whispers: *She's a witch, she's a witch!* It's possible that the spirits of the cemetery were picking up on Linda's gifts, and interpreting them in a decidedly nineteenth-century way.

This was not the team's only contact with cemetery spirits. During the trip to Decatur, the team also explored a local graveyard as well as the Culver House. As they walked through the graveyard, the recorders picked up an EVP of spirits whispering, *They're leaving ... they're walking away.* Unaware of this, Linda had just had an idea.

"I remember I told Debbie, 'I think I might have figured out a way to pray for these people. What if we bring a candle back here, and we light it? And because there's no time or distance, we can pray for them then.' And on the recorder, you can hear excited voices whispering, *She's coming back!*"

This happened over and over again. Linda would hear voices coming through over the recorder after many investigations. *Look, it's Linda ... Linda's here ... hey, it's Linda...* Linda didn't know who these voices belonged to. At the time, she assumed they were spirits needing help. "We had the right people with the right talents. We heard these EVPs from the very first day we went out together." The voices called out first to Linda, then to Beth. Then they named Libby, and even Jerry, Linda's husband.

"We went to one old lady's house in Roanoke. As we were doing the investigation, my car alarm started going off. The spirits were trying to separate us. We got out to my car, and I still had my recorder running. As clear as a bell, you could hear *Jerry! Hey! Hey Jerry!* and you could imagine someone standing there, waving their arms, trying to get my husband's attention."

There was a lot of activity going on in that house in Roanoke. Linda says that there was a chandelier on the house with space in the fixture for a dozen small bulbs, but there was only one bulb screwed into its socket. But that one small bulb managed to light up the entire room – it shone that brightly.

And that wasn't nearly the limit of the weirdness in that house. Linda says that in the room with the chandelier, the lighting would go from brilliantly lit to the roiling dark shadows of an approaching thunderstorm. "This blue light would come down, and you could see visions. One was of a woman kneeling beside the bed, as if she was praying. There was the face of a man, and the face of a small boy. You'd be standing in the bedroom doing an EVP session, and knocks would come from the closet behind you.

"This was an amazing house. There was so much going on. We were investigating in the basement of the house, and right in front of me, a tall, thin, black substance appeared. It was *right* in front of me. I said, 'Would you mind moving? You're in my way.' And it did, it moved away a little bit. I was filming, using the camera on my phone, and my team members have seen that film. And when we were in the basement ... it was dark, and we were standing around talking, and I could *feel* the presence in that house. I asked my friend, 'Could you hand me a flashlight?', and I put my hand out for it. My friend gasped, 'I didn't even know you were standing there!' It turned out that I was totally blacked out, completely hidden by this dark mass. It was in front of me, blocking me, and my team didn't even see me. They didn't know I was even in that part of the room until I stuck my hand out for the flashlight. Then they saw my hand come out from behind this blackness."

Even after Central Illinois Ghost Hunters visited the house, the strange visions continued. "The guy that lives in the house still talks to the spirits," Linda says. "He'll say, 'Give me some sign that you're here,' and he'll hold up his cell phone and snap a picture. And he'll just get the most phenomenal pictures."

Linda and her group worked together at that time with a very clear purpose: to help people who were experiencing the supernatural – and were terrified by it.

13. CENTRAL ILLINOIS GHOST HUNTERS

"We were very blessed," Linda says of the original group that made up Central Illinois Ghost Hunters. "We had a unique mixture of people with specific gifts. I don't think it would have worked separately.

"Because we worked so well together, it was either the perfect blessing or the perfect storm, depending on how you look at it. From the very first time we went out, we got EVPs just as clear as anything. We would hear these things, and we'd look at each other in astonishment and we'd say, my goodness, we've got better stuff than the guys on TV! Where's this coming from? The flashlights would turn on immediately when you asked the spirits questions.

"We had good techniques, too. We were all professional, trustworthy. Once we left that motorhome to begin an investigation, the recorders were on. They went on the moment we stepped outside the camper, and we left them on even when we came back to the camper to regroup. We'd catch things even inside the motorhome, because the spirits would follow us in to talk to us. We took it seriously, and we treated our cases with integrity, confidentiality, and professionalism. We had the perfect team to bring about some amazing things. We made an excellent group. What one person didn't do, another person did. It was wonderful."

And what this group did was investigate the supernatural – and they did it nearly constantly. One October several years ago, they did thirteen investigations in a month. The group was out practically every weekend night, many times working until the wee hours of the morning. Sunday afternoons were reserved for house cleansings and sending spirits to the Light. Add to that the time spent after the investigation, listening to recordings for evidence, staring with gritty eyes at the video screen. Ghost hunting can be a very time-consuming hobby. But the group kept at it. Their expertise was in high demand.

"There are so many people out there that need help. People would come to me saying that things were happening in their house, that their children were scared.

They'd say, my child is too terrified to sleep in their room because of the knocking, or the voices, or the shadow man standing next to the bed. People called us for help. Many times, they had called their pastor or priest – and many times the priest refused to come to the house, either because they didn't believe the people, or were too busy, or just because they didn't want any part of it. We were it, we gave these people hope that *someone* was willing to listen to their stories."

The stories certainly were out there. Central Illinois Ghost Hunters ended up doing forty-nine cases in one year. They were busy every weekend, and sometimes during the week.

Right away, the group discovered a sobering fact. People lie. The first question in their investigation was always the same: have you ever been involved with the occult – witchcraft, séances, things like that? Have you ever played around with a Ouija board? These are the things the investigating group needs to know right from the jump. And of course, the answer is usually "no" – at least up front.

There was a case in Bartonville which involved two children. The eight year old girl couldn't sleep in her downstairs bedroom. The baby, in an upstairs bedroom, would also wake up screaming. Linda walked into the girl's bedroom and was assaulted by a disorienting spinning sensation, as though a vortex was swirling around her. "We all felt it. It felt like the whole room was spinning. We literally had to touch the wall to get our bearings." The investigators also experienced a dark heaviness in the baby boy's room, and the basement was crawling with spirits. Some of these spirits were aggressive.

Sometimes, on an investigation, you can feel the touch of the spirits. Investigators have described it as feeling like the flutter of small insects or spiderwebs on your skin. Linda felt that strongly in the basement of the house in Bartonville, and it nearly knocked her out cold.

The fluttery feeling hit her all at once, all over her face. "I felt like the spirits planned this. I kept rubbing them off my face. They were all over my face, even on my eyes. I couldn't see, I couldn't concentrate. I said, 'I've gotta go upstairs.' Well, the basement's ceiling was very low, and in my hurry and confusion, I walked right into a low beam. I cracked my skull a good one. I think the spirits were hoping I'd seriously hurt myself."

The next day, Linda got a phone call from the children's mother. "Oh, I forgot to tell you," she said airily. "I had a deck of tarot cards in a drawer in the hallway right across from where the baby sleeps."

Linda fought down a surge of irritation. It was possible, she supposed, that the woman had honestly forgotten about the cards. "Still, when someone asks, Have you ever? you really should be able to answer the question truthfully."

Another case, this one in Metamora, brought home the importance of discovering all of the background to a case. This is the only case at which Linda has been physically ill. She managed not to throw up, but she couldn't stand to be in the house.

It wasn't only the feeling of nausea that bothered her, either. She couldn't stand to be near the owner of the house, the client who had called the group for an investigation.

"It's like he scratched my spirit. It was like sandpaper rubbing on my soul. Every time he came close to me, I would just want to scream. Our motorhome was command central for our cases, so that we could travel together, and discuss the cases on our way home. I did not want this man in my camper. I didn't want him touching anything I owned."

The whole house had an odd feel to it. The group got an eerie feeling just walking through the rooms. And as they started down into the basement, Linda was hit with a god-awful stench, like nothing she had ever smelled before. The nauseating reek permeated the air, and she felt her stomach roil in protest.

"I was thinking, oh my gosh, if I don't get out of here, I'm gonna throw up in this basement. And the funny part was that my group smelled it upstairs. Everyone else smelled something foul upstairs, and I couldn't smell a thing. But when we started to go down to the basement, I was overwhelmed by this stench, and no one else noticed it."

Linda beat a hasty retreat to the motor home. For the next hour, even in the safe confines of the camper, she could catch rank whiffs of the nauseating odor.

The group found out later that evening that the client, the man whose presence felt like sandpaper on Linda's spirit, was a practicing devil worshipper. He boasted of having done a money spell, and his technique had more than a whiff of witchcraft to it. "I lit candles in a circle," he said. As he explained it, each candle had a purpose – and the last one was "supposed to belong to him", meaning the devil. "But I kept that one," he bragged. It was as if he thought he'd pulled one over on the Prince of Darkness, and was proud of it.

"He called me later, trying to get me to come to his home again. Said his kids were having problems, and could I come out? I told him to sprinkle every corner and door lintel of his house with holy water and salt, to renounce all his association with Satan, and to anoint his children's foreheads with the holy water too. Well, he didn't reply to that. He wasn't about to put holy water on his children. Instead of replying, he just snickered, 'Are you scared to come out?' I said, nope."

During this hectic time, Linda and her fellow investigators noticed something unsettling about the spirits they were encountering on their cases. One popular method of paranormal investigation is the flashlight technique. A flashlight, with fresh batteries, is placed on a level surface. The investigators unscrew the lens of the flashlight almost all the way off, so that the barest touch is enough to make the connection between the light bulb and the battery. Then they back off, sitting several feet away. They ask questions in the hope that the spirits will use the flashlight to communicate – turning the light on for "yes", for example, then turning it off to "reset" it for the next question.

"They got to be … a little obstinate, for lack of a better word. They wouldn't turn the light off as fast, when we asked them to. It's like they were acting differently around us. At first I thought, well, the spirits must be getting stronger.

"It never dawned on me that I was getting weaker."

Central Illinois Ghost Hunters was in high demand. The group travelled in a 150 mile radius, taking cases as far away as Springfield and Shelbyville. It fell to Linda to review the evidence. This meant sitting at the computer for ten, sometimes twelve hours a day, listening to hours upon hours of recordings in the hopes of catching a snippet of EVP (electronic voice phenomena, or the voice of a spirit caught on tape).

The group would drag home in the achingly small hours of the morning. Linda began skipping church on Sunday mornings. She knew it was a mistake. She was a staunch Christian, and she believed firmly that without worship and fellowship to feed her soul, she would get weaker. "Just like you feed your body what it needs to survive, you need to feed your spirit – especially when you're dealing with the unknown. Because who is your Protector?"

But the late weekend nights were taking their toll, and it felt so good to sleep in and recover when she had the chance. Even so, Linda realized she needed to start going to church. But before she could, CIGH got called out to another big case, this one in Pekin.

14. "AH'M WAITIN' ON YOU": THE STONE CIRCLE

"I believe that God knows exactly what we're going to do, from the day we're born throughout our whole life. We have freedom of choice, we have free will. But I believe that whatever choice we make leads us down a different path. I had a feeling about this case, and I should have listened to my intuition."

Linda had been growing increasingly dissatisfied with her work as a paranormal investigator. The cases just didn't hold her interest the way they had done in the past. And she was getting tired of her clients lying to her. It seemed that in nearly every case, people would swear they'd had nothing to do with the occult before calling CIGH in for an investigation, when actually, they'd toyed with a Ouija board, or shuffled a deck of tarot cards. Then, belatedly, they'd confess it to Linda and the team. Linda felt that this behavior was putting her team – and her clients themselves – in danger. In fact, she was seriously considering giving up being an investigator altogether.

The only pull the cases still had for her was in the possibility of clearing the house of its resident spirits. The other investigators could play with their cameras and their meters and their recorders. Linda just wanted to "pray the house out", telling the spirits to leave. "If they were good, I wanted them to go Home. If they were bad, I wanted them to go away. That became my goal. I just wasn't interested in flashlights going on and off anymore."

Two weeks before the investigation in Pekin, Linda had come to a decision. She would turn the leadership of Central Illinois Ghost Hunters over to Beth. But unbeknownst to her, Beth had been having the same feelings, a suspicion that she needed to leave the group. Beth and Linda had always had a strong bond, and Beth was unconsciously picking up on Linda's distress.

There were other distressing circumstances as well. CIGH investigated the Pollak Hospital, on the grounds of the Peoria State Hospital in Bartonville. While in the basement, Beth had run into the dark entity that makes its home in the morgue. She cannoned out of the basement and tore up the stairs. When she rejoined the rest of the group, she said flatly, "I'm not going back down there." She hasn't been back since. Beth wouldn't give any details about her experience. All she would say was that she had seen a huge black mass, and that it scared her to bits. That was the moment she decided she wanted out.

Beth had another reason to leave the group. She wanted to have a baby. After much soul-searching, she had decided that ghost hunting and caring for an infant were activities that didn't belong together. She wanted to protect her young family from paranormal weirdness.

The week before Linda planned to tell the members she was leaving, Beth dropped her bombshell. Spirits were low, feelings were bruised, people were confused and hurt. In the middle of this upheaval, which would end up rocking CIGH to its core, the group was called to an old Victorian home in Pekin.

This was another house with strange vibes, with lots going on – both spiritually and in the physical world. An extended family lived there. In addition to the dad, mom, and their two children (a three year old girl and a baby), there was also the children's aunt and her five year old daughter in the house. The grownups were all quite young, all in their mid-twenties.

"This is what bothered me most of all that last year," Linda says. "The first year the group went out on investigations, the cases involved adults. The last year, many of the cases involved children. It was children who were hearing voices, children who were seeing apparitions ... children who were getting scared."

Linda and her group came up the sidewalk, carrying case after case of equipment. The young woman opened the door as the ghost hunters climbed the porch steps. As the investigators snapped the latches open on each hard-sided suitcase and started to set up their equipment, the woman told a familiar story, of dark feelings in the house, of the children having trouble sleeping in their rooms at night.

Linda and her team would soon discover that there was more – much more – to this house than a simple haunting.

The team did a walkthrough of the house, deciding which rooms to concentrate on during the investigation. They exchanged uneasy glances as they got closer to the door that led into the basement. There was *something* behind that door, down those narrow stairs – something unpleasant. They could all feel it.

"My daughter … she keeps wanting to go down there," the young mother of two spoke up. The three year old girl was inexplicably drawn to the basement. She was fascinated with her daddy's workshop, and often begged to go down to the basement to "help".

More disturbingly, the toddler said there were people who called her down to the basement.

Linda and her team members checked their equipment. Each investigator carried a DVR, or digital voice recorder, a small machine used by students to take notes in class – or by investigators hoping to catch a ghostly voice in the recorder. The red "recording" light on each DVR glowed as the group made its way down the stairs.

The basement was a dark, dank, unfinished room. The dirt floor crunched softly under Linda's shoes as she led the way further into the basement.

"There's some kind of structure down here," she spoke for the record. "It's a low stone wall that forms a circle, right here in the basement. There's a door that leads into this circle … weird."

"We don't let our daughter go into that circle," the mother said. "It's like she's drawn to it. But I'm afraid to let her actually go in." She shivered.

Linda nodded. "That's smart. It's weird, but I'm getting kind of a voodoo vibe from this place." Other team members nodded in agreement. Later, when Linda listened to the audio files, she heard a black woman's voice on the recorder, her accent sultry and syrupy with the languid tones of the deep Old South.

C'mon down … Ah'm waitin' on you.

Unaware they were being watched, Linda and her team put a flashlight down on the dirt floor in the middle of the stone circle. "Turn the flashlight on for 'yes', please. Then turn it off so we can ask another question. Do you understand?"

The flashlight's beam flickered to life in the darkness.

"Starting the EVP session … were you into hoodoo or voodoo?"
YES
"Were you a slave?"
YES
"Did you practice your religion down here?"
YES
"Are you wanting this three year old child for something?"
YES
"Are you after her soul?"

YES YES YES

The flashlight stuttered on and off in response to the questions. The "YES" answers also showed up on the audio recording that the video camera picked up. The voodoo priestess, though, wanted to be sure the investigators know exactly with whom they were dealing.

"This was one powerful lady. When we were down there, at the stone circle, every one of us had a recorder. I looked around, and every red light was on. We were down there thirty, thirty-five minutes. When I went back to listen to the recordings, that whole section ... nobody's recorder picked it up. It started at the top of the stairs – there was no part of what we did in the basement that came out. It was like it was erased from everyone's recorder, because none of them caught it."

Oblivious to the priestess' presence for the moment, the group wrapped up their recording session in the basement and headed back upstairs. Further strangeness awaited them in an upstairs bedroom. The spirit of a little girl came to the group – a little girl who knew far too much for her years. She had her own ideas about their methods of speaking with the dead.

The girl seemed to be speaking with the voodoo priestess whose powerful presence haunted the basement. The young spirit's voice dripped with scornful amusement.

"Oh, Auntie, they can't SEE us ... they're just kidding!"

In conversations with the family, the spirits' methods of haunting and seduction came out. Chillingly, they would show themselves to the little girl in the form of her father.

"They would come into her room in the middle of the night, and it would be her daddy. He'd say, come with me, honey, let's go down into the basement and play."

Once, this happened in broad daylight. One Saturday morning, the father had gotten up early and was relaxing with some cartoons on the couch. About seven or eight in the morning, the little girl came trotting down the stairs, scampered over to the couch, and grabbed his hand.

"Come on, Daddy, let's go!"

"Go where?" the father asked, puzzled.

"You told me it was time to go play in the basement!"

A prickle of unease crawled down his spine. "No, honey, I didn't tell you that."

"Yes you did, Daddy!" the toddler insisted, her brow furrowed with the effort of making him understand. "You came upstairs, and you said come on, let's go!"

The investigators exchanged glances when the father shared this story. They were shocked at the brazen attempts of the spirits to lure the child down to the stone circle. The father was concerned for his daughter's safety, but the mother, a skeptic, refused to believe the story.

Linda couldn't hide her shock at the mother's stubborn refusal to believe what her husband was telling her. "It's no different than a child predator, even if you can't see it. Something in this house wants to grab your daughter. What better way for it to gain the child's trust than to pretend to be her daddy?"

The parents had been down in the basement, watching as the flashlights stuttered on and off in response to the team's questions. They were intrigued at this proof of the paranormal. As the team was leaving that first night, Linda gave them a stern warning.

"Under no circumstances should you let your daughter go down there. There's something evil in that basement, and it wants your little girl. You've seen that. Don't let her go down there."

Even that warning couldn't quench the parents' curiosity. Over the next several weeks, they invited friends over to the house, just to show off the stone circle and its spirits. They took flashlights down with them, and treated the whole situation like a party game. Maybe they were after a cheap scare ... but they were still encouraging the spirits that lay in wait within the circle.

Some time later, Linda came back to pray out the house and bless it, in an effort to rid the place of the evil within. The parents of the three year old were willing to have the house cleansed. Linda went through the house, praying and sprinkling salt and holy water in every corner and on every window sill.

The aunt, who also lived in the house, was present for the house blessing. She stood by nervously, chewing on a hangnail as Linda spoke the Lord's Prayer and invited the spirits in the house either to go Home or to leave the house in peace. When she had finished, the young woman came up to her.

"Linda, can I show you something?" she said in a low, urgent voice. "I keep hearing my uncle calling me. He's ... he's been dead for a while." Then she pulled up her sleeve.

Angry red gashes stood out on her pale skin. She'd been cutting herself. Tears stood in her eyes as she gazed at Linda.

Linda winced at the sight of the cuts. Something she'd heard on the evidence tapes suddenly made chilling sense. She had heard voices saying, "*Let's get Cassie. Let's get the aunt.*" The spirits were calling out to Cassie by name, and she was terrified.

Within a month, the young woman was dead.

She had gone out to the garage to smoke a cigarette. When she didn't return, her five year old daughter went out to get her. The puzzled child came back into the house moments later.

"Mommy's asleep and I can't wake her up."

Cassie was twenty three years old. Her cause of death was listed as "unknown".

As terrifying and disturbing as that case was, it wasn't the only warning Linda and the team got during that time. Something big was brewing, a battle for souls, and the fighting in the spiritual plane was beginning to spill over into the physical world.

The members of the group were noticing that their cases were getting stranger and stranger. No longer were they just investigating your standard "creepy feelings after dark" hauntings. Activity was ramping up – and Linda and her team were right in the middle of it.

One of the investigators, Debbie, got violently ill while at a house in Peoria, for no reason at all. This was the second time CIGH had been to the house. They had done an investigation, and later came back to cleanse the house. The atmosphere in the house on that second visit was very heavy. It was all they could do to concentrate long enough to say the Lord's Prayer. The team put blessed salt on all the windowsills, above the window frames, and on the door lintels. Every entrance had to be sealed and protected with blessed salt and holy water. In the camper on the way home, the team was listening to the recordings, and they caught an entity saying, *Whew ... I'm glad we got them out of there.*

During the investigation, the team heard something even more chilling.

"We heard the spirits talking. They said, '*You take Debbie* [the investigator who had gotten sick], *and I will guard Linda. The Dark One wants Linda.*'" Linda believes that these voices belong to guardians, angels that were charged with protecting the group.

On that same case, Central Illinois Ghost Hunters captured a very strange EVP. It wasn't a voice, or a scrap of ghostly humming or whistling, or the bang of a door or the thump of footsteps.

It was the unmistakable metallic scrape of a sword being pulled from a sheath, then the clashing strike of metal against metal. Was a spiritual battle being fought, unseen by the humans in the house?

At the same investigation, Linda was doing the preliminary walkthrough, and was in the bedroom with the owner of the house. Linda laid her hand on the bed. Her fingers tingled as a curious vibration thrummed through them. She turned to the woman, realization dawning on her face.

"They sit on your bed!" Linda blurted.

The woman nodded. "That's right. They sit on my bed and they look at me." "They" were dark, nasty, ugly little imps ... tormentors, according to Linda.

The bedroom was the room in which the investigators had caught the sound of the sword being pulled from its sheath. There's nothing in the world that makes quite the same distinctive metallic cry. It's a sound of danger, of menacing authority. "I could almost picture a guardian angel standing there, saying, 'Kid, you're way off track being in this house with all this evil, but by God, we're gonna protect you no matter what,'" Linda says.

"There was horrible darkness in that house, just horrible," she recalls. "But whatever was in that house, we were being protected. Something was most definitely protecting us."

Yet another house held dark surprises for CIGH. This was a beautiful, sprawling home in the countryside outside of Mackinaw. The owners were business people, wealthy and well-respected in the community. But even this privileged, upper-middle-class family couldn't escape the darkness that entered the house on the night the kids decided to have a séance.

"CIGH got called to the house because sometime after the séance, something invisible slammed into the sliding glass porch door so hard that it cracked the glass," Linda says. During an EVP session, she asked, "Are you the one that broke the door?" and got a *yes* in response. The entity also snarled "*get out*" at the group.

While at the house for the investigation, Linda felt something slip past her with a chill whoosh of air as it headed for the dark refuge of the basement. The owner of the home actually saw a dark shadow pass Linda at that moment. The team came back later to cleanse the house. It was on that second visit that Linda saw, just for a split second, a huge black figure in the house.

"It was tall – well over seven feet – and it was standing there with batlike wings furled at its shoulders." Linda described the entity to the homeowner. The owner confessed that the mailman had seen a similar figure at the house. The menacing apparition scared the mailman so badly that he quit that rural route, pleading for an assignment in town.

In the midst of all that supernatural activity, Linda was still neglecting her church attendance. When you're doing case after case, running all over the area investigating hauntings, helping people who are terrified to stay in their own homes, it's easy to give in to the lure of a comfortable bed on Sunday morning ... especially if you've just gotten to sleep several short hours before. Sunday afternoons were devoted to house cleansings. "The spirit is willing but the flesh is weak"-- how well Linda was finding that out. She was tired. She was worn down from the constant adrenaline press of investigations, and she hadn't been to church in weeks.

Linda would soon come to regret her lapse. Sheer physical exhaustion, spiritual drought, and mental frustration were about to come together in a perfect storm, one that would affect Linda and her family for years to come.

And it all started with a sincere, but woefully misguided prayer.

15. "LET HER HEAR": THE ATTACK

July 2012. Linda yawned as she turned the key in the front door. Sunrise would come much too early, but for now, the warm night enveloped her in shadow as she set her equipment bag down just inside the door. She'd unpack that afternoon, when she had the oomph to start tackling yet another investigation's worth of evidence. It was exciting enough, especially with all the activity they'd been getting in recent weeks. But the thought of sitting there listening to twelve hours of audio files – to say nothing of watching several hours of video hoping to catch a fleeting glimpse of the unexplained – just felt like more than she wanted to think about just then. All she wanted at that moment was to tumble into an inviting bed and lay her head on her cool, soft pillow.

Linda shut the door behind her, then turned to face her living room with a sigh. So much had happened in the past few months, and she was still trying to process it. Not the evidence – she'd been through that several times already. She'd heard the voodoo priestess' syrupy Southern drawl – *"C'mon down ... I'm waitin' on you"* – and the little girl's scornful observation – *"Oh, Auntie, they can't see us! They're just kidding."* She had heard the tall, bat-winged entity's snarled *"Get out!"* She had heard the scrape of metal on metal as something drew an invisible sword – for defense, or for attack? She didn't know.

No, it wasn't the evidence that bothered her, as fascinating – and disturbing – as it was. Linda's background had prepared her for the strange and the unexplained. But her heart still ached for those affected by the hauntings ... the living who suffered with the unknown, and the lost souls who wandered Homeless through the shadows of the afterlife. Her mind flitted from case to case, unable to settle on a single thought. It was simple exhaustion, she knew that ... but no matter how she tried, she couldn't get the thoughts out of her head.

That little girl ... so young, and yet so worldly, Linda thought. *If only I could understand her better. And what about poor Cassie? Hearing her dead uncle's voice ... cutting herself to escape – what? And then she's just gone ... twenty three years old, and she left behind her young daughter. Could I have done more somehow to help her?*

The desire to help, to *do* something, overwhelmed her. Right there, in the living room, Linda opened her heart and prayed.

"I made the mistake of praying," Linda says. "I figured that if I could hear the spirits, I could help them right then and there. But the Lord had quite a different plan. The Lord said, Do you really want this? Because I'm going to show you what this really is. I'm going to take you on this journey."

In her living room, Linda spoke aloud, praying from her heart. Her voice shook with sincerity and exhaustion. "Father, I think that I could help them more if I could hear them. Please, let me hear them."

Instantly, Linda heard the sweet tinkling chime of a small bell. It was the melodious sound of the bell the altar boy rings in the Catholic Mass at the moment of transubstantiation, when the host is consecrated. Then a Voice said: *"LET HER HEAR."*

Immediately, Linda heard three voices – two male, one female – shrieking around her head. She clapped her hands over her ears in horror, but the screaming continued.

Linda's first instinct was to pray. She cried aloud, "Oh God, I'm so sorry! Forgive me for asking to hear this – I don't want to hear it! I did not know – I thought I was asking to hear little kids who were lost. I didn't think I'd hear *this*! It was not my intention, Lord. I don't want to hear evil." But her abject apology went unanswered.

"They were screaming in my ears constantly from then on. They would say the most horrible things – '*We want your soul*', '*Worship Satan*', really awful stuff. They would taunt me, accusing me of doing these horrible things – things from my past, things I had completely forgotten about. They would scream at me, saying You did this, you did that, you're a worthless, horrible person. And these were things I had done *years* ago."

The demons railed at Linda constantly, in loud gruff voices that scraped at her mind. They accused her of long-forgotten sins, blowing up trivial offenses from her childhood all the way up to the present. The abuse was horrific and unrelenting.

"These things knew everything that I had done since I was a little kid. It goes along with my Christian teaching, which says that there is a book in which all of our deeds are written down. Lucifer stands before God and accuses us constantly. How can he accuse us if he doesn't know everything about us? These demons could tell me everything I had ever done wrong in my entire life, even things I had forgotten that I had done. Fortunately for us, Jesus stands at God's right hand and acts as an intercessor."

But in this case, the Lord's intercession was silent. The demonic screaming filled Linda's head and blocked out nearly everything else.

"They were tormentors. These things were screaming at me while I was trying to sleep. I didn't sleep more than four or five hours a night for a month, because they were constantly haranguing me. I could easily understand how that would drive someone insane, if they didn't have faith."

Even through the haze of abuse, Linda realized that the demons had limitations. She would hear one gibber, "*Bind her. Kill her!*" Then another one would snarl, "*We can't – she's protected.*" From this, Linda knew that the demons could torment her, but they couldn't take her life.

That was cold comfort, though, as she struggled to get through daily life with a trio of demons loudly spitting poison in her ears. "They know everything about you, all your mannerisms, all your secrets. They know the funny way you squint your eyes when you're upset. They know that when I get nervous, I start singing. They know when you are scared or confident, or loving, or at peace, or terrified ... they've had years to study us – not only us, but our families as well."

Linda's family was at a loss. Her husband, Jerry, had only an inkling of the torment Linda was going through. And her kids had no idea why their mom was suddenly acting so strangely.

"I was out to lunch with my daughter one afternoon. I stood it as long as I could, the abuse, the shrieking. Then I politely said, 'Danette, please excuse me a minute,' because these things were screaming in my ear while I was trying to talk to my daughter. I went to the restroom, locked myself in a stall, and prayed with all my might.

"I prayed, 'God, You say we are saved by the word of our mouth and the word of our testimony. I love you, Father God. I choose You, the Father and the Holy Spirit. I *always* will choose you. I want no other but you. That is my word and my testimony. I wrap it up and I lay it Your holy altar, because you say that whatever we say goes right to your throne. Lord, I lay it at your feet. I only want you. I *only* want you. Please, please help me through this.' I was crying, begging, pleading in that bathroom stall."

Danette was understandably concerned at Linda's strange behavior. She called Bobby, her brother, to tell him that something weird was going on with their mother. Bobby is a businessman, an entrepreneur, a very logical, no-nonsense guy.

"Mom, I'm a little concerned about you," he said. "Do you think you might need to go to a psychiatrist?"

"Bobby, if your own child broke his leg, would you take him to a gardener?" Linda shot back. "I don't need to go to a doctor. I need spiritual help. This is a spiritual battle, and I need to find help within the church."

In her gut, Linda knew that a trip to the psychiatrist's couch would only end badly for her. She knew this was a spiritual problem, not a mental issue. Any psychiatric doctor she saw would most likely have prescribed medication for her, and she instinctively shied from that. Any medication a doctor prescribed would likely have helped her to sleep. That much was true. But even so, Linda feared that the demons might have found a way to pierce the haze of sleep and torment her anyway. And she knew without a doubt that with her defenses down due to being medicated, the abuse would have been much worse.

"I knew I could always call on the Lord, and I did. I would say, 'You promised me that you wouldn't let me go beyond what I could withstand – and I can't stand this.' I begged for help." This plea would bring her a moment of peace. It bought her just a few minutes of breathing room before the torment started up again.

Linda actually did see a doctor during those first few terrifying months, but it was not done as a concession to her son's concern. Dr. Sebastian, the family's physician, is a Christian himself, and a paranormal investigator. He and Linda would trade ghost stories back and forth. None of Linda's tales, though, could have prepared him for her revelation.

"I told him that I had three evil entities tormenting me day and night. To his credit, Dr. Sebastian never offered me any drugs. He didn't even suggest it. He just said, 'Linda, I will pray for you.' I was in such anguish, but I was so grateful that God had given me good people to pray for me, to give me the spiritual strength to get through all of this."

Linda decided to keep a journal of her experiences, just so there would be a record of what she was going through. She opened a notebook, picked up a pen, clicked it ... then thought, *wait a minute. Why should I give them credit?* She bent over the notebook and started writing.

Those things woke me up screaming last night, but God is greater.

She refused to let the demons win.

16. SEEKING HELP

"*WAKE U-U-U-UP!*" a rough voice screeched a grating sing-song in Linda's ear. Her eyes flew open and she sat bolt upright, her heart pounding and her fingers tingling with the sudden adrenaline dump. In the darkness, she could hear the gibbering screams of the three demons. Next to her, Jerry slept on, oblivious to the cackling shouts. Linda shot a despairing glance at the clock on her bedside table.

The glowing numbers read 2:38.

Linda buried her face in her hands. She was so tired. She ached all over, but it was her mind and her heart that hurt the most.

"Leave me alone!" she moaned. She didn't want to wake Jerry – why should he have to suffer too? – but she couldn't just lay here in her own bed and take this abuse. The demons giggled and chattered –

She threw back the covers and got out of bed. She reached for the robe that hung over the back of the chair and pulled it on. Trying to ignore the shouted threats of the demons, she glanced over at Jerry, still sound asleep. *How can he possibly sleep through all this?* Linda's mind supplied the answer with a pained wince.

He can sleep because he doesn't hear the screams. It's not him they're tormenting. It's me.

Linda shuffled to the living room and collapsed onto the couch. She reached for her phone, checking to see that she'd plugged it into the charger before bed. With her mind still fogged with sleep, she thumbed in a number she very nearly knew by heart now.

The phone on the other end rang three times, four, five, six ... then a sleep-muddled voice answered. "H'lo?"

"Mike, it's Linda. I'm so sorry –" She was nearly weeping with frustration and embarrassment – "but they woke me up again." She could hear the demons now, like the high maddening whine of a mosquito that evades every slap.

"Shh," the voice soothed. "I'm here. I'll pray with you."

Linda had gotten Mike's name from a friend. Mike is an exorcist who lives in Wisconsin. When Linda contacted him, she asked tearfully, "Can you help me?"

"Absolutely," came the reply. "I'm here for you. Call me any time, day or night, and I will pray with you."

"They'd wake me up in the middle of the night," Linda says. "It wasn't that I couldn't sleep – they'd scream me awake. Two, three, four o'clock in the morning, I'd call Mike. He'd talk to me on the phone for hours."

The demons wouldn't leave her alone, even when she was in the middle of a phone call. Mike knew the demons were horning in on the conversation, so he would acknowledge them, trying to learn more about them.

"Ask him – what's his name?" Mike said at one point.

The demons could listen in just as clearly as someone eavesdropping on a conversation. One of them snarled, "*Tell him I don't have to answer him. He's not even an ordained minister.*"

Linda was shocked into silence. She'd had no idea Mike wasn't ordained – she had just assumed he was. After all, he was an exorcist, and they were priests – right?

"What are they saying?" Mike urged.

Still reeling, Linda relayed the message. "They're telling me that you're not a real exorcist. They're telling me you're not even an ordained minister."

Mike was silent for a long moment. When he did reply, his tone was stilted. "It doesn't matter if I'm ordained or not," he said stiffly.

"That was a shock to me, and I could tell he was clearly flustered," Linda says. "Mike had simply been given approval by the deacon of his church to carry out his helping ministry. But no, he had no special dispensation from the church to perform exorcisms. The spirits knew this. The supernatural realm knows far more than we do."

Faced with these staggering odds – three demons with the flames of Hell behind them against one human woman – Linda at first did the only thing she knew how to do.

She tried to fight back.

Linda is a born fighter. She is easy-going, slow to anger, but if she is backed into a corner, she will fight. The spirits knew this about her, because they had watched her from the day she was born.

"I yelled at them. That was my biggest mistake, acknowledging them. They seek attention. They crave it. It would have been better just to start praying immediately, as soon as they started yelling."

The consequences of this defiance were severe. Linda said she feels that she had to deal with the entities for much longer, as a result of trying to fight them instead of surrendering in prayer.

But Linda is a scrapper. "I started to wonder – how can I fight back? How can I defeat them? Can I ignore them, can I yell back, can I try to deceive and trick them, to divert them somehow? I was actually trying to use my own strength, which seems laughable now. It was probably like a game to them. These things are eternal. How do we stand against something like that? We don't stand a chance on our own."

But Linda kept on fighting. When the demons would start their shrieking, she would yell back. "Leave me alone! Leave me alone. I am a child of God – leave me alone!"

The demons would scream their challenge. "*You belong to us. I am your god!*"

"Leave me alone," Linda begged. "I cover myself in the blood of the risen Christ. You have to leave me alone!"

The demons would lay low for a while ... but they'd always come back.

The voices weren't always gruff and loud, dripping with venom. Sometimes, they sounded just like normal conversation. "When they wanted to torment me, that's when they would shriek in my ear. But sometimes they talked at just a normal level. I could hear them all the time, and it was like they were playing a game with me – I was their mouse. They knew what they were going to do, and they knew full well that I could hear them. They would talk to each other, as if they were talking about me behind my back. They'd say snide, sneaky things like, '*Is she listening to us? I don't know... D'you think she can hear us?*' But they knew. If I tried to think about other things, or if I started to pray, they'd get louder and louder and louder."

It was while hearing the regular voices like this that Linda came to realize there were three entities, two male demons and a female. The Devil, in his arrogance, loves to copy God. Thus the appearance of three demons to torment Linda, in a grotesque parody of the Holy Trinity. Even the pleasant, silvery chime of bells that Linda heard at the start of her persecution was a way for the Devil to thumb his nose at God. He used the sound of bells, which signal the holiest moment of the Catholic Mass, to announce the beginning of his torment. "Was that bell necessary? No," Linda says. "It was just for dramatic effect. The Devil likes to do things with flair. They feed on that stuff. Their main desire is for attention – look at me, look at what I can do."

The most insidiously evil of the three demons was a spirit that had the arrogance to call himself "Michael". Saint Michael the Archangel is the four-star general of God's army, a powerful protective spirit, a champion sworn to defend God's children against Satan and his minions.

David Lowery, also known as The Paranormal Highwayman, is one of two "Volunteers in Residence" at Ashmore Estates, and a seasoned paranormal investigator. He is a great bear of a man who is totally at ease with the supernatural. For years, he has been concerned about evil influences that might affect ghost hunters. "I've never really come across anything, but now, whether that's a function of just not finding anything, or whether my protection is so good, I don't know."

The most important thing, David says, is to believe in your protection. "I chose Michael as my protector years ago. It seems to work for me."

And David doesn't wear his respect for Saint Michael on his sleeve. Instead, it is permanently etched into his flesh, a constant reminder of the Archangel's presence in David's life. David sports a full-color tattoo of Saint Michael on his upper right arm. The detail is incredible – the warrior angel, clad in blued steel armor, stands victorious over his adversary. Satan is crouched in defeat, about to slide off into the reddish-orange flames that lick the edges of the eternal chasm. Michael's wings are flexed, he's just dealt Satan the final blow, and the power and sense of responsibility he feels for God's servants radiates from his handsome face.

"My daughter has a lot of tattoos, and she started going to a very talented tattoo artist in Springfield [Illinois]. When I decided to go gung ho with the supernatural, I figured I ought to get some protection. The artist and I went over so many designs – he said, 'You're my best friend's father, I *can't* mess this up!' He really captured Michael well.

"Angels in art are always kind of cherubic. They're very strong and muscular, especially the warriors, like Michael. But they still have the smooth, handsome faces and the flowing curly hair."

Shortly after he had the tattoo done, David suffered a simultaneous brain stem stroke and heart attack. David spent weeks in the hospital, fighting his way back from the brink of death. There are pictures of him lying in his hospital bed, the Michael tattoo blazing in a wealth of color against the stark white of his gown and sheets.

"I give credit to Saint Michael for getting me through that too. I think he's a protector, not only against evil, but just in general, for all life situations."

Many religions acknowledge the warrior angel. He is part of Jewish, Christian, and Islamic teachings. He has been a protector of the church since the time of the Apostles. Sanctuaries dedicated to the saint first appeared in the fourth century, and by the sixth century, Michael was an intrinsic part of both the Eastern and Western churches. He can be found in the lore of Roman Catholics, Eastern Orthodox, Anglicans, and Lutherans. Michael is widely venerated across many religions ... and with good reason. The archangel is a powerful and trusted protector.

I asked David about the demon's masquerade as Michael. "How could someone tell the difference between an angel and a demon trying to pose as an angel?" I asked.

His opinion is that demons – true demons – are incredibly rare, contrary to what popular culture would have us believe. Horror movies can have us thinking that there are devils under every bed, when in fact, they are not that common.

Part of the rite of exorcism is demanding the demon roll over and give up its name. David says that a demon will avoid identifying itself directly if at all possible. When an exorcist knows a demon's name, he can then order the demon – by name -- to leave its human host.

As for Linda's faux-Michael, David says, "Posing as an angel ... that's a new one. I've never heard of a demon pretending to be an angel before – but yeah, they are certainly capable of it." There is professional interest in his voice as he speaks. But there are other ways of telling if you're dealing with a demon, or just "a really bad head-ghost", as David's daughter likes to say. His advice in such a situation is simple and intuitive.

"Call on the *real* Saint Michael. In your prayers, explain what's going on. Tell him you need a sign that it's really him. The real Archangel Michael *will* protect you."

The Jehovah's Witnesses have a slightly different interpretation of Saint Michael. Rather than seeing him as a saint, or even an archangel, they consider Michael to be sort of a glorified form of Jesus.

There is a prayer to Saint Michael that is incredibly effective. Pope Leo XIII wrote it in 1884. He was inspired, so they say, immediately after being allowed by God to hear a conversation between God and the Devil. On October 13, 1884, he collapsed during a Curia meeting. While comatose, the pope was granted a vision of Hell and of Saint Michael defeating Satan in a fierce battle. When he recovered, he grabbed a pen, ink, and paper, and wrote the exorcism prayer as a tribute to the warrior angel. "*Saint Michael the Archangel, defend us in battle. Be our protection against the wickedness and snares of the devil. May God rebuke him, we pray, and do you, oh prince of the heavenly host, by the power of God, cast into Hell, Satan and all evil spirits who prowl through the world seeking the destruction of souls. Amen.*"

In our own time, Pope John Paul II encouraged the use of this prayer as well. The pontiff actually performed an exorcism right out in the open, in St. Peter's Square, in September 2000. A young woman had come to a public audience with the pope. She sought his help personally, going straight to the top. She had suffered through two exorcisms performed by the renowned exorcist Fr. Gabriele Amorth, but those rituals had done nothing to give her relief from her demonic torment. The pope himself prayed over the woman for half an hour, and was finally able to banish the demon, albeit temporarily. This was, in fact, Pope John Paul II's third exorcism. Satan is indeed alive and well in the twenty-first century.

When David was investigating the Pollak Hospital on the grounds of the Peoria State Hospital, he and his team members were down in the morgue, and some nasty spirit found them. David's videographer Carrie was filming in the basement, and something attached itself to her.

"Something got ahold of her and made her deathly ill. She had to go outside and vomit several times. Even when we got back in the truck to go home, she was still very sick. I said, okay, this is enough, and I called on Saint Michael. I said the prayer, and sure enough, whatever it was let go, and Carrie was fine all the way home. All it takes is an experience like that to convince you that Saint Michael is a powerful ally."

Linda has her own personal relationship with the archangel.

"Years ago, I had the most amazing experience. This was before I nearly drowned, so I must have been about fourteen. At that time, I had very vivid dreams that came true, right down to the smallest detail. I remember one night, I was sound asleep, and Michael the Archangel came to me. This is why I say that God knows what's going to happen to us before our lives even begin … Michael held a key in his hand. He took that key and he pushed it into my heart, and he said, 'Linda, no one can take your essence unless you give it to them.' I've never forgotten that. No one can have my soul unless I give it to them."

The demons knew of Linda's relationship with the powerful angel warrior. One of them subtly insinuated himself into her life, impersonating the archangel to give Linda a false sense of security.

"I truly believed that I was doing God's will, that I was helping people who had sought help from their priest for a paranormal problem. I thought I was showing them that someone who loved the Lord God could stand against the forces of darkness. I wanted to save their children from torment. At times, when I was talking with clients, trying to get to the bottom of their distress, I could feel strong, feathery wings enveloping me. If I was wearing short sleeves, I would feel the 'archangel's' feathers brush my arm."

Even after the three demons started tormenting her, she would still feel a strong presence that she interpreted, at the time, as Michael. "It was as if, when the spirits were harassing me, Michael would step in to say, 'It's all right. You're all right, you're safe.'"

It was at this time that Linda got in touch with Father M., an exorcist in the Quad Cities. In her desperation, she sought out anyone who could possibly help her.

"I went to see Father M., who was the exorcist for the diocese of Rock Island. You don't just go in and talk to these people. You have to go through a bunch of rigamarole – but he was retired, which is how he was able to see me."

Linda's two visits to Father M. sound like a scene from the middle of a horror movie, but without the special effects. It just didn't play out that way. Father D. had introduced her to Father M., and brought her to the exorcist's home. When Linda and Jerry arrived, they were ushered back to a room that had been prepared for Linda's exorcism. Candles glittered in red votive holders, and wisps of incense wafted in the air. Father M. took a deep breath, picked up a small leather bound book, opened it to the satin ribbon marker, and started to read the rite of exorcism.

And nothing happened. Linda didn't vomit pins, or levitate, or experience anything out of the ordinary – except for the mocking voices of the demons ringing in her ears. The first rite took about forty-five minutes, with Father M. chanting in Latin as the candle flames flickered. But Linda knew immediately that the rite hadn't worked.

"He read the rite of exorcism over me, but it didn't do any good at all. Father M. was surprised, but I could tell it just hadn't worked, because the demons were still tormenting me. There's a huge difference between possession and oppression. He's reading from the book while they're all around me screaming in the background. He couldn't hear them. I'd tell him what they were saying, and he was just amazed."

Two weeks later, still seeking relief, Linda went back to the Quad Cities, back to Father M.'s home. Again, he read the rite of exorcism, and again, she went away disappointed. The rite had failed ... again.

During this visit, Linda told Father M. that the Archangel Michael was protecting her from the influence of the demons. Father M. immediately corrected her: "No, he's not. That's one of the demons. He's hiding behind the holy name of the archangel. He's probably the worst of the three."

Linda gasped as she realized the deception. After all, what better way to trick someone than to pretend to be a trusted confidante? She thought back to the house in Pekin, where the evil spirits had taken the form of the little girl's father to lure her down into the basement to the stone circle.

I wondered how the priest could be so immediately sure of this. Linda pointed out that, well, he is an exorcist. He has a strong gift of discernment that is a great help in his exorcism work.

This was the beginning of months of frustration, as Linda sought help. At the time, she was going to church daily, and sometimes twice a day. "I'd go to St. Thomas in the morning. Then I'd go to Sacred Heart for the noon mass."

At one point, she went to a Catholic charismatic gathering. Dick was Linda's prayer partner at the time. The two had met when Linda first became interested in converting to the Catholic faith. Dick suggested that they go to the Thursday evening meeting of the charismatic group, held at St. Viator's in Peoria.

The group met in the basement of the church. There was one woman in particular, an older woman, that Dick wanted Linda to meet. Dick came down the stairs with Linda, scanned the room, and nodded.

"See that lady sitting over there? That's Rhonda. She has actually been through an experience similar to yours."

Dick led Linda across the room to Rhonda, who looked up at their approach. "Rhonda, this is Linda. Would you be willing to pray with her? She's going through a tough time right now."

Rhonda hesitated, then reluctantly, she agreed.

"She came over to me, and she said, 'In the name of the Lord Jesus Christ!', and she touched me with the flat of her palm, right on the forehead. I went right to the ground. It knocked me off my feet, even though she had just barely put her hand on me. She said, 'You ugly, lizard-like demon!' Everyone else kind of looked around, like what's going on, you know? What's happening here? So when I got up, I made the mistake of telling her something.

"The demons were clustered around me, and they snarled, 'Tell her we're gonna come see her tonight!' I told her that, and it scared her to death. It scared her to death, because she had just gotten free of all that, and here these things were threatening to visit her. She left immediately. She told Dick, 'Don't give her my phone number. I don't want anything to do with her. I cannot be involved in this.' I was upset by this. I had the feeling that if she hadn't been so afraid, we could have been friends."

After this deeply personal rejection, the other members of the group gathered around. They told Dick, with a certain amount of regret, "We can't lay hands on her. We can't pray for her…she needs to go see an exorcist." They feared a sort of spiritual contagion, a threat posed by the demons that tormented her.

Linda was hurt by the group's rejection. She was raised to believe that every member of the Church has gifts, including the power to pray for the afflicted. It's the responsibility of the churchgoer to "stand up without fear", and accept those duties to care for their fellow parishioners. "It says 'do not fear' in the Bible something like 367 times. The Bible says we need to go around preaching, healing, baptizing, and casting out demons. We need to take these duties seriously – we can't cherry pick our ministry. I knew that if they would just believe, and just … not fear, and if all of them would lay hands on me, these things would be gone. But they were scared to touch me. They were afraid it was going to jump to them."

Linda understood their fears. But at the same time, she was deeply frustrated – and hurt by their rejection. "If you are a member of a Catholic charismatic movement, and you claim these gifts – the gifts of healing, of casting out demons – you should use them. You shouldn't draw back and refuse to help, out of fear. If they believed in prayer and healing, then why wouldn't they pray for me?"

At the same church, Linda spoke with several of the priests. Their reaction was nearly as disappointing as the charismatics' unreasonable fear. Their solution was simply to shake her hand and say piously, "We'll pray for you, Linda."

Linda was aching with frustration. The priests, to whom she had come for help, were keeping her very real problems literally at arm's length. Linda was not raised in the Catholic faith; she converted seven years ago. But she was raised Christian. She grew up in the belief that if you are having problems, you kneel before the altar. A priest kneels with you. He lays hands on you and he prays with you for victory over your struggles. Linda knew she needed someone to lay hands on her, and it frustrated her to be put off with a simple handshake.

At the same time, she had gotten no relief from the exorcists. When the Charismatic group suggested she undergo yet another exorcism, she fumed as she tried to explain her situation.

"I am not possessed. They're not inside me, they're around me. They're oppressing me. Your rite of exorcism isn't going to do me any good."

The Catholic Church didn't know how to handle a case like Linda's. The exorcists of the Church are trained to cast demons out of people. They are at a loss when it comes to dealing with demons who are *around* someone, not *in* them. Exorcism is for possession cases. In cases of attachment, like Linda's, exorcism simply doesn't work.

The monsignor at St. Viator did give Linda a bit of good advice. Linda told him about the demons, how they screamed at her and abused her constantly. "Monsignor, these things are just yelling at me all the time."

The monsignor's response was simple and well-meant. "Don't stop looking for help, Linda. That's what they want you to do. Whatever you do, don't stop looking."

17. "FATHER, DON'T FORGET ME!"

One morning, the voices around Linda's head were particularly bad.

"*We want your soul, we're gonna take your soul!*" they gibbered as Linda held her throbbing head. Linda groaned aloud with the torment. Oh God, why? Why was this happening to her? She knew Jerry couldn't hear the demons' cries, but that wasn't much comfort right now. Linda groped for the phone and scrolled through her contact list to the Ds.

"Dick, these things are just screaming at me," Linda said as soon as her prayer partner answered. "I need prayer. Please, Dick, I need your help."

"Honey, come over to where I'm at," he said. "I'm at a remodeling job. I'm working on a house with two other guys who are believers. Come over here and we'll pray for you."

Linda grabbed her purse and stumbled towards the front door. Hearing the jingle of fumbled keys, Jerry looked around the corner.

"Hey, hold on just one second! You're in no shape to drive. You're half out of it now, for Pete's sake! Where do you think you're going?"

"Dick said he'd pray for me," Linda whimpered. "He's at a house ... he gave me an address…"

"Let me take you," Jerry interrupted. "Give me those keys."

Linda let her head rest against the cool glass of the passenger side window as Jerry drove out to the address Dick had given her. The demons were still shrieking abuse at her, but Jerry calmly took the corner, peering at the numbers of the houses they were passing.

"Here it is," he said, relief flooding his voice. "And there's Dick."

Linda yanked the door handle open and tottered from the car. Dick gave her a quick hug, and held a phone out to her. "We've got a priest on the phone. He's the head of an abbey in Peoria, his name is –"

Another man grabbed the phone. "I know who that is. He's a good friend, he'll help you out." He spoke into the phone. "Father? I got someone here who could really use your help."

Linda gave Dick a despairing look. A demon crooned savage whispers in her ear, and she shook her head fiercely, trying to get rid of the clotted voice. "Do I get to talk to this priest, or what?"

Dick sighed. "That's Al Smith. He's kind of a ... take-charge kind of guy. Don't let him get to you."

Linda closed her eyes. She wanted to talk to this priest, whoever he was, she really did. But Al had the phone to his ear, talking a mile a minute. She'd be lucky to get a word in edgewise – if the priest didn't lose patience with Al and hang up on him first, she thought.

Dick took Linda's elbow and bowed his head. "Our Father, who art in Heaven ..." The other man chimed in, repeating the ancient words of comfort. Linda felt the tightness in her chest ease fractionally. Maybe, maybe this time things would turn out all right –

"*Gonna take your soul! You're LOST!*" the demons screamed. Linda yelped and reached for the phone, taking it from Al in mid-sentence.

"Father, please. You don't know me, but I really need your help."

Al frowned, and reached for the phone again. "You're pretty rebellious," he grumped as he took the phone from Linda's sweating hand. "You need to be more submissive." He put the phone to his ear and started talking to the priest again, as Linda felt her blood pressure rise.

"See, Father, what's going on is that this lady here, Linda, she says her name is, she's having all kinds of trouble with demons, really bad spirits. That's what she says, anyway. Says they're screaming at her all the time, like when she's trying to sleep and pray and things."

Linda reached for the phone again. She didn't care any more about being rude to this Al fellow. He was testing her patience, and right now, with the female demon snarling in her ear, she had no patience to spare. She wrestled the phone from Al, ignoring his squawk of protest. She gripped the phone tightly, trying to resist the urge to turn on Al and rip him a new one. If the demons would just SHUT UP for a moment, just for a second so she could THINK –

"You have a problem being quiet," Al snarked.

"As do you," Linda snapped back. She had a chance to talk to a priest, and she wanted him to hear that she needed help desperately. She prayed that the priest would listen to her. All she wanted was for him to listen, just listen ...

In the background, Linda heard the sweet sound of bells. Dimly she remembered Dick saying something about this priest being at an abbey. Was that the sound of bells at the monastery? Was the priest being called away already, just when Linda had finally gotten to speak to him?

"I'm sorry ... I have to go," the priest was saying. "I have to take care of my duties here. I have to go."

Desperately, Linda wailed, "Don't forget me, Father! Please ... don't forget me!"

18. FATHER JOSE REYES

On November 19, 2011, Father Jose Reyes, OSB (Order of Saint Benedict), was installed as the abbot of Saint Benedict's Abbey in Peoria, Illinois, the second man to hold that title in the abbey's then-26 year history. Fr. Jose is a tall, handsome man who carries himself with the assurance of a born leader.

Born in New York, Fr. Jose moved to Puerto Rico with his family at the age of seven. He was raised Roman Catholic – his parents attended church faithfully every Sunday. Fr. Jose himself served as an altar boy, and went to a Catholic high school. He will admit, with a wry grin, that as he grew older, he didn't always behave as he should have done.

"There was peer pressure, yes," he says. "I went to my share of parties, with dancing. I know it doesn't sound terribly scandalous in this day and age, but back then, that was skating close to the edge of what was proper."

His conversion to a truly religious life began when he was a senior in high school. "All of the seniors had to go on this retreat. That's when I started to look at people for spiritual reasons, and not just for their appearance. I became friends with a classmate of mine. I hadn't noticed her before then, because she wasn't really pretty. But she became my best friend."

This classmate told the young Jose about another upcoming retreat, this one focusing on charismatic renewal. Jose went – but he was in for a shock.

"I went expecting the retreat to be Catholic … but this looked more like Pentecostal!" All around him, people were raising their hands in worship, and singing their praises. And there were further surprises in store. The next retreat featured a music ministry, where the participants sang in tongues.

"That was the first time I heard angels," Fr. Jose recalls. "I still get goosebumps remembering that, even after thirty years."

These retreat experiences fanned a flame in the young man, a desire to serve God. Before that, he had planned to become an accountant.

"The Catholic school I attended in Puerto Rico was middle- to high-class. It was seen as demeaning to stay in Puerto Rico. Everyone wanted to go to the United States, to attend a prestigious college. Out of my class of seventy students, we have several doctors, politicians, and engineers. One of my classmates spent twenty years working at MIT, then went straight from there to NASA. That's where he works now."

Jose was accepted at Saint Vincent De Paul University in Chicago, where he joined a youth group. However, he was not inclined to join the Vincentians. A friend suggested that he study at Dominican University and concentrate on philosophy, the better to prepare himself for entering the seminary. Jose was to visit many religious communities over the next couple of years, as he searched for his spiritual home. In

1985, in his third year of university, he visited the Abbey of Saint Benedict in Puerto Rico.

"The abbey was founded on August 15, 1985, and I came to the abbey that October. At the Abbey, I found everything I was looking for. There were four things I wanted out of any community I joined. I wanted prayer, holiness, and formation, and I wanted a community that was devoted to the Virgin Mary."

Father Jose joined the Benedictines at the Abbey, and settled into life in the monastic community. In the mid-1990s, great change came to the Abbey.

Sadly, it came in the form of religious persecution. Puerto Rico is a small island, and the Abbey soon found itself in constant struggle with the bishops of the Catholic Church. The Abbey is "ecumenical within the Catholic tradition", which means that it is open to worshippers from every Christian denomination. But it is independent, and that ruffled some feathers.

"Being an Ecumenical community, we didn't have support from the hierarchy of the Church. The monastic life itself has its own challenges, so if on top of that you add outside struggle with the Church, the monks really begin to have difficulties.

"A person that is seeking to fulfill their vocation in the monastic life would find it very difficult to concentrate on that vocation while also having to deal with church politics. We lost a lot of members because of this. At one time, there were eighteen monks at the Abbey. When we moved, we were down to four.

"There is a whole process to becoming a monk. There are different levels – you start off as a postulant, then move up to novitiate. Then you become a junior monk, where you've professed what's known as simple vows. You stay at that stage for three years, as you decide for yourself if the monastic life is something you really want to do. After that three year period, you become a solemnly professed monk, and that is for life. We lost people at every one of those stages, whether it was novices who just didn't stay, or monks who made their simple vows, but didn't go on to make their solemn vows because of all the struggles that were going on."

The Abbey kept losing members, and the remaining monks eventually decided to move to "the mainland." The monks had contacts in several states – California, Illinois, New York, and Florida. They began a process that would stretch on for about two and a half years. They would visit the States for a week or so, travelling and looking for property that would suit their needs. Then they would return to Puerto Rico to ruminate over what they'd experienced. Six months later, they would make another seven-day trip, and keep on looking.

On their visits to the States, the monks would either stay at hotels or in people's homes. In Illinois, they stayed at a house in Peoria. The lady of the house was a Mexican woman who was married to a Puerto Rican. In preparation for opening her home to the visitors, she had been praying to God to send Puerto Rican priests to the area.

"That's very specific," Fr. Jose notes. "That's not 'Hispanic priests', that's not 'American priests who speak Spanish'. It's not Columbian, Venezuelan, Dominican ... you can go on and on through the entire list of South American countries. She specifically asked for Puerto Rican priests ... and here we are! We took that as a sign from God that this is where God wanted us to be. We obey God – He tells us to do something, and we do it. We don't know all of the reasoning behind it, we just follow His lead."

In 1996, the monks bought property outside of Peoria, a parcel of rolling green nestled in the hills of the Illinois River valley. They soon settled into their new home in the heart of Illinois. The Abbey is very active in charity work, especially in feeding the hungry. They get groceries from the Peoria Food Bank, and frozen sandwiches from HOI Vending. Then they act as sort of a clearing house for the distribution of the food. Churches from Pekin, Galesburg, even as far away as Princeton come to the Abbey and collect food for their own parishioners who may be in need.

In this, they follow the guidance of their patron, Saint Benedict. In his Rule, the saint wrote: "Then they are real monks, when they sustain themselves by the work of their hands."

This idea of sustainability differs from abbey to abbey. Fr. Jose told me of some of the larger European monasteries, with populations of a hundred monks or more. There's a monastery in Germany that keeps cows and chickens for its needs, and they sell meat, eggs, and cheese in their gift shop. The monk in charge of the livestock actually holds a degree in animal husbandry. There are monasteries that are their own little towns, with their own train stations along the rail line. There are monasteries, even in the United States, that are devoted to teaching. The monks there teach at the university attached to the abbey, and the head abbot is also the headmaster of the school. Many of those abbeys also tend to be retreat centers, so there are large facilities dedicated to the pursuit of solitude and peace.

Fr. Jose and the other monks settled into the quiet life of the abbey. Other men joined the community, and the tiny group slowly began to grow. All was well ... until about 2001.

"I spent about eight years suffering from fibromyalgia. I had tests done in 2006, and I got a bit of relief, because they'd found out that I was allergic to a whole bunch of foods. In men, fibromyalgia is mostly due to food allergies. But by 2009 I was living in constant pain, twenty-four seven. I could find absolutely no relief."

A priest, Father Giotto, had been invited to do a healing service at the abbey. The service had been set up by another priest, and Fr. Jose decided to meet with Fr. Giotto himself, to settle on details for the service. He'd never met Fr. Giotto, but he satisfied himself through testimonials that the other priest did in fact have a healing ministry.

When Fr. Giotto arrived at Saint Benedict's, Fr. Jose sat down with him and with Bishop Morales, who was the abbot at the time. The three men spent several hours talking about the upcoming healing service, and about Fr. Giotto's healing ministry.

At the end of the conversation, Fr. Giotto announced that he wanted to pray for Fr. Jose and the bishop.

"I hadn't told him about my fibromyalgia. We hadn't discussed anything personal at all. Our conversation had centered mostly on planning the healing service. Fr. Giotto had told us about his experiences in the seminary, and about receiving the gift of healing from God, but that was it."

The three men went into the Blessed Sacrament chapel and knelt before the altar. Fr. Giotto prayed aloud for the bishop first. Then he turned to Fr. Jose.

"He asked me two questions: What do you want from Jesus? And, do you believe that Jesus can do it? At that time, things with the fibromyalgia were deteriorating. I was also starting to develop neuropathy. I was experiencing extreme pain in the joints of my hands and feet. It hurt me to walk. I asked God to heal me of that pain – that's all I asked for. I really didn't ask to be completely healed of the fibromyalgia. It just didn't occur to me."

Fr. Giotto began a form prayer, then paused in mid-sentence. "I'm getting that you're suffering from a herniation between L4 and L5 [the lumbar discs of the lower back]."

"As soon as he said that, I started to smile," Fr. Jose says. "I believe in the charismatic renewal, and the gifts of the Holy Spirit manifesting. I believe in the gifts of prophecy, knowledge, and healing. As soon as he said that, I knew: this is real, this is from the Holy Spirit. There is no way he could have known this."

"You're having immune system problems too," Fr. Giotto continued. Again, Fr. Jose nodded: yes.

"I closed my eyes," Fr. Jose recalls. "When I did that ... okay, have you ever seen the Tom Cruise movie *Minority Report*? Where they have the computer screen in the air in front of him, and he swipes his hands in the air to change the readout on the screen? It was just like that. Things were being removed from my records, things that were wrong with me. As this was going on, we prayed. We prayed not only for healing, but as things were removed, we prayed that God would fill those voids with His peace, love, and virtue.

"I felt instant healing that night. I don't know how to explain it, or how to describe it. I just knew, in that moment, that I was healed."

The way fibromyalgia messes with the immune system, in men, is that the body interprets certain foods as irritants. "It was easier to say what I *could* eat, instead of listing what I couldn't. Basically, I could eat meat and vegetables. That was pretty much it. I was allergic to pasta, egg – yolks *and* whites – dairy, wheat and gluten both ... I was allergic to soy, too, so any alternatives were out."

On the day Fr. Giotto prayed for healing for Fr. Jose, everyone went out that evening to Olive Garden. One of the candidates who was planning to enter the monastery was celebrating his birthday, and the monks all joined him for dinner at the restaurant. That night, Fr. Jose had pasta with cheese and Alfredo sauce – lots and lots of dairy. He savored every bite.

"I suffered from migraines too, just like my mother does. Her doctor said, no chocolate. Whenever I got a migraine, I'd look back on what I'd eaten that day, and more often than not, I'd had chocolate."

For dessert at the restaurant, Fr. Jose chose a piece of triple chocolate fudge cake.

"It had been so many years that I'd been on a restricted diet, that when I sank my fork into that cake and brought the first bite to my lips, I was nearly in tears, it tasted so good."

After that healing experience, Fr. Jose started working with Al Smith, who was a member of Friends of Martha Ministry. Fr. Jose began praying for people that Al would bring to his attention. "I had so many experiences – I'm so privileged to be an instrument of God. One woman I helped started to cry as she realized that my gifts were from the Holy Spirit. But honestly, I couldn't have known the information any other way.

"And it is temporary. It's not like I walk around getting vibes all the time. Even when I pray for people, I don't always get this knowledge. I've learned that in cases like this, since I'm dealing with a God who cannot be controlled, it's best for me to just get out of the way. It's not about me … the more I put of myself into the situation, the more difficult things become."

Fr. Jose is quick to point out that there are different degrees of demonic attachment. "True possession is very rare. It involves the person voluntarily inviting the demon into themselves. That's the key – the demon has to be invited in, it can't come in without an express invitation. Oppression is much more common. Most common is demonic influence."

Fr. Jose uses the book *The Rite* as an example – the book that was later made into a movie starring Anthony Hopkins. "The priest in the book studied in Rome for a year to be an exorcist. What he did, mostly, was pray over people, and then send them on their way. He told his mentor, I'm confused – where are the manifestations? He only saw three or four in a year. But think of it this way: if you're doing this for four hours a day, Monday through Thursday, you're seeing hundreds of people in a year. If you only see a handful of true possession cases in that time, that tells you how rare it really is."

He has, however, had his own experiences with evil. "I had a woman come to the abbey for help, who said she actually felt something coming out of her as we prayed, something that felt like lots of rage." And when he lived in Puerto Rico after his conversion, he attended a prayer service for a man who was involved in spiritism.

Fr. Jose had gone to a place of pilgrimage. The Virgin Mary was said to have appeared at the site. A church had been built there, and the faithful came regularly to pray.

"There were about thirty or forty people standing around in a circle praying for this man. The outer circle was praying the rosary, and the inner circle was praying more specifically. It felt a whole lot like an exorcism. The man was jumping up and down, kind of uncontrollably ... you could tell he had no control over his actions. They had the guy reading scriptures, and he would distort the reading, and not want to finish. They put the Bible in front of him to read, and his speech was slurred and broken. He sounded like someone who was being controlled. They wanted him to read a certain passage, 'that at the name of Jesus every knee should bow, in heaven and on earth and under the earth, and every tongue declare that Jesus Christ is Lord, to the glory of God the Father' [Phillippians 2:10-11, NLT (New Living Translation)]. He couldn't say those words. He would turn his face from the Bible. They were ordering him to say those words, and he wouldn't say them. Then he'd start convulsing again."

The deliverance took several hours. "I had actually come to the church to visit as a pilgrim. I had no idea that people had gathered to pray for this man. I stayed for a while, then I left to walk around the grounds and visit the site of the apparition of Our Lady. When I came back, hours later in the evening, the group was still praying."

Fr. Jose heard later that the priests took the man into the church and displayed the Blessed Sacrament, and that's what finally drove his demon away. They opened the tabernacle and displayed the consecrated Host. When the Eucharist was exposed, there was a loud shriek – and that seemed to be the end of it. The man stumbled out of the church on the arms of the priests, weak from his ordeal, but okay.

It's important, too, Fr. Jose says, to discern the difference between spiritual difficulty and mental illness. Psychology is an important component of his ministry. "I look at patterns in the person's life," he says. "You have to pray for discernment and guidance as you talk to the person. We do much the same thing when we talk with a man who wants to join the brotherhood at the Abbey. It's sort of like a personality test, to make sure they're suited for the monastic life."

Fr. Jose has seen his share of the supernatural. He has experienced healing miracles. He is a Benedictine monk – and the order is proudly autonomous. Every Benedictine abbey is its own self-contained community. Fr. Jose is self-assured, confident, and strong in his faith.

But even this warrior of God would find himself rocked by what was in store.

19. "THIS IS LINDA K., AND I NEED HELP"

Linda's friend Donna works as a counselor at Antioch Counseling, and had been a missionary to Thailand. After months of demonic torment, Linda called her in a panic.

"Donna, I know you believe in these things. I know you've seen things on your mission trips. I know you know this is real, and that I'm not crazy. These things are really tormenting me. Do you know anyone that would pray for me? Please, please help me get through this, or give me direction as to what I need to do." Linda had been praying constantly, trying to fight the demons that harassed her. But it was so hard to concentrate with the entities screaming at her all the time.

By this time, Linda was desperate. She had been to seven priests, and had undergone two exorcisms. She felt as though she was rapidly running out of options. Where can you turn, when everything you've tried has failed?

"This is how the Lord worked," Linda says with a serene smile. "Donna, bless her heart, had made a mistake – but that mistake led me where I needed to go."

Donna called Linda one day. "Linda, I'm so worried about you, and I'm praying for you all the time. Listen, there's a monk who comes in here, into the counseling center, every day to say prayers for us. He's a little monk who dresses in brown – I think he's from Saint Benedict's Abbey."

"This was Donna's mistake," Linda explains. "The monks who live at Saint Benedict's dress in black robes, not brown. So the monk who was coming to Donna's church was *not* from the Abbey ... but God used Donna's words to lead me to the Abbey. This planted the idea in my head to call the Abbey. I needed help, and I needed it fast."

During a respite in the demonic torment, Linda dialed her phone with shaking fingers.

"This is Linda K., and I need help. I'm in a battle for my life. This is spiritual warfare, and I need your help."

The voice on the other end of the line was calm, unexcitable, the very sound of serenity. "Come see Father Jose tomorrow at one o'clock."

"All right. I'll do that." Linda hung up, her heart pounding. Could this possibly be the avenue of help for which she had been searching?

The next morning, Linda and Jerry went to the ten o'clock Mass at Saint Viator's in Peoria, the same church that played host to the charismatic group that had pushed Linda away so forcefully. Linda had been trying to go to Mass every day, trying to feed her spirit, to fight the entities.

"During the Mass, I couldn't sit still. The demons were screaming at me. I was in a battle for my life, I needed my spirit fed, but I just couldn't stand it anymore." The spirits, perhaps knowing that Linda had made plans to visit the abbey that afternoon, had stepped up their assault on her psyche.

Linda, her ears ringing from the abuse being shrieked at her, swung around to face Jerry. "I cannot wait until one o'clock to go see this priest."

"But your appointment's at one," Jerry protested.

"I don't care," Linda pressed, trying to ignore the yells of the demons. "If you don't want to sit there with me, that's fine. I don't care if you drop me off and leave me, I will sit there outside the abbey until one o'clock. Drop me off. Leave me. But I can't wait. I have to go there now. I can't explain it, but I *have* to go there now."

Jerry shrugged. He couldn't hear anything, even when Linda winced and clapped her hands over her ears as she did sometimes. But he trusted his wife. He stood, and, excusing himself, started to move down the pew, dodging knees as he went.

Gravel crunched under the tires as Jerry braked to a stop in the driveway of Saint Benedict's Abbey. He turned the key, and the engine quit. Silence fell – silence that Linda couldn't appreciate. For her, there was no silence.

"We own you! Say it – admit it! We're your god now!" The howls of the demons were relentless. Linda scrabbled for the door handle, yanked the door open, and nearly fell out of the car in her hurry to get out. The sun was shining brightly, but she barely noticed the morning's beauty. She had to get into the abbey. She *had* to see the priest, this Father Jose. The voice on the phone told her to come.

The gate to the courtyard opened, and a man came out. He was dressed casually, wearing shorts in a nod to the summer weather. He was whistling tunelessly to himself, tossing a bunch of keys in the air and catching them. He looked as though he didn't have a care in the world.

He's going to think I'm a crazy woman, Linda thought. She was willing to take the chance. She ran to the stranger.

"I need help," she blurted. "I have an appointment at one o'clock with Father Abbot, but I need help now. I can't do this, I need help now."

The man stopped, and peered at the babbling woman. For a long moment, he just looked at her, his head tilted in mild curiosity.

"Oh-kaaaay," he said. "Go over to the church. I'll go get Fr. Jose."

Linda didn't know it, but the man dressed in shorts and a t-shirt was Bishop Morales. The bishop has the gift of discernment. "He knew those things were around me. He could see them."

Linda stumbled up the wide stairs to the church and pulled the door open. She saw a small office to her left, and went in. Gratefully, she sank into the upholstered chair. The peach-colored walls were soothing, and a picture of Pope Francis smiled down at her. She breathed in the faint scent of candle wax, and felt the tension in her soul ease slightly. The three demons were still railing abuse at her, but she concentrated on the smell of the church and the feel of the soft chair underneath her.

The key-tossing man appeared at the door of the office, knocked softly at the open door, and came in. He was followed by a tall man, whose black hair was cropped close to his head, and whose closely trimmed goatee was slightly flecked with gray. The second man wore the black robes of a monk. Linda leaned towards him, drawn by his air of gentle strength. Maybe one of these men was the monk whose voice she had heard on the phone yesterday, the one who had calmly said, "Come see Fr. Jose at one o'clock tomorrow."

The key-tossing man said, "This is Fr. Jose, and I'm Bishop Morales. Now, how can we help you?"

Linda poured out her story, ignoring the outraged shrieks of the demons. It felt so good to tell! Now, maybe, she could finally get some help. Engrossed with sharing her story, she barely noticed when the bishop slipped from the room.

"And I tried to get help from the charismatic group at the church I attend in Peoria. I asked Dick – he's my prayer partner – for help too, and he had some men praying for me at a house he was remodeling. Complete spur-of-the-moment thing, but that's the story of my life right now." Linda gave the man a nervous smile. Would the monks here be able to do anything, anything at all?

Fr. Jose had been sitting quietly, listening to every word. He rubbed his temples absently. The supernatural energy swirling around Linda was giving him a headache. Now, though, he stirred in his chair. His eyes widened in sudden recognition.

"You're the one who said, 'Father, don't forget me!'"

Linda nearly burst into tears. "Are you that priest? Are you the one I talked to that day?"

"Yes, I am. When you said that, it went straight to my soul. I have never forgotten that. I have been praying for you every day – *every* day."

Bishop Morales knocked on the office door again. He was no longer the casual, key-tossing stranger Linda had seen when they had driven up to the abbey. Now, he was dressed in his liturgical garments. He was ready for spiritual conflict.

Fr. Jose stood up and gave Linda his hand. "We're going to help you," he said, his voice ringing with confidence. "Let's go."

Fr. Jose led Linda across the hallway to a small chapel. There, Linda knelt in front of the altar. Bishop Morales laid a cross on Linda's head, and Fr. Jose put his hands on her head as well. She was dimly aware that Jerry had joined them, and was sitting quietly in the corner of the pew behind them. The two monks began to pray.

"Heavenly Father, I love you, I praise you, and I worship you. I thank you for sending Your Son Jesus Who won victory over sin and death for my salvation ... let the healing waters of my baptism now flow back through the maternal and paternal generations to purify my family line of sin. I come before You, Father, and ask forgiveness for myself, my relatives, and my ancestors..." Linda read along with the Spiritual Warfare Prayer as the two men intoned the words.

Suddenly the bishop paused in his reading and looked up. "Linda, there's a little boy here with us. He's attached to you. He loves your maternal instinct, your caring, your protectiveness of spirits that need help. But you need to tell him to leave, to go to the Father right now. You have to tell him that the Father will take better care of him than you ever could."

Linda closed her eyes, her heart swelling. Even with all the pain the paranormal had caused her, she still instinctively ached to help lost spirits. "Honey, go to the Father. He will take care of you, He will love you. You will be with family that you've never known. You will be safe and loved and protected, and you will never be afraid again."

All three of them, Linda, Bishop Morales, and Fr. Jose, have different experiences of what happened next. The bishop saw a young boy's soul flit towards the altar, headed towards the Holy Sacrament. Linda and Fr. Jose saw the child's spirit drift quickly up to Heaven, joining the spirits of the just. And all three of them heard a child's sweet voice say, *Thank you.*

Linda gasped. "He said thank you!" Tears stood in her eyes. She had helped one final spirit make his way to the Light.

"I heard it," Fr. Jose said in a hushed voice. The bishop added, "I heard it too."

Linda closed her eyes, still feeling the warmth of the men's hands on her head. The demonic voices were finally stilled, distant whispers for the first time in months. She felt as though she could see a light at the end of the tunnel. She felt released from her torment.

She felt free.

20. "I THOUGHT I WAS SAFE!"

Linda continued to battle the three entities that still tormented her. She still had a long struggle of several months ahead of her. But the intercession in the Blessed Sacrament Chapel – the very same chapel in which Fr. Jose was healed of his fibromyalgia – was a turning point for her. She knew instinctively that the laying on of hands was what she needed to break the stranglehold of the demons. She needed to kneel before the altar, to pray along with the priests, to be surrounded by prayer.

Linda became a regular visitor to the Abbey. She started going to Mass there, overjoyed to share her spiritual journey with people who understood what she had been through over the past year.

Fr. Jose was still stunned at the amazing confluence of events that brought Linda to the Abbey. He told me his version of the story.

"Al Smith was a member of the Friends of Martha Ministry [the group, incidentally, that provided the copy of the Spiritual Warfare Prayer that broke the demons' hold on Linda]. He would pray for folks who needed it, and he would let me know if any of them needed my help as well. This woman had come to a house where he was working with a few other guys. They were praying over her, and Al called me on the phone. I talked to this lady for about an hour and a half, I guess, but then I had to let her go. I had other duties to attend to. She said, 'Father, please don't forget about me.' That touched me. That went straight to my heart. I said, 'I will not.' I started praying for her every single day.

"About a month or so later, she showed up at the abbey. We weren't expecting her at all. She said the weirdest thing … she said, 'Father, I know we have an appointment at one, but I just couldn't wait that long.' In the back of my mind, I was thinking, I don't really know who you are, and I'm sure we don't have an appointment! But a vow of charity dictates that we help those who need it, and she was obviously in some sort of distress. Honestly, I didn't know what she needed.

"But as she told us her story, I suddenly made the connection – this was the same woman from the phone call a month and a half ago.

"Sending spirits to the Light is a serious thing to do. It usually needs sanction from the Church. You really ought to have spiritual backup in such a situation. It can be dangerous to do on your own, even if it's well-intentioned. It's like moving someone after an accident; it can sometimes do more harm.

"But I did want to pray for her in the presence of the Blessed Sacrament. We went to the chapel, where we would be in the presence of Christ. We spoke the Spiritual Warfare prayer – Father Giotto uses this prayer often as well.

"I was so glad that Linda felt immediate relief with this prayer. The Spiritual Warfare prayer binds curses, hexes, spells, that sort of thing, even back to the third generation. Any mistakes our grandparents made, even unknowingly, are bound and extinguished by this prayer."

But Linda's struggle wasn't yet over. Bishop Morales and Fr. Jose gifted her the cross that the bishop had laid on her head at the beginning of the prayer. She wears it all the time now, trusting the power in the blessed object to keep the demons at bay. She even wore the cross to bed for a while. That decision turned out to be unwise.

"They threatened to strangle me with it in my sleep. I wore it to bed, thinking that maybe, the spirits wouldn't scream me awake in the small hours of the morning, like they'd been doing for months. They'd shriek, 'Take that thing off, or I'm gonna choke you with it.' But they would grab the cord and pull it tight, trying to choke me, cutting off my air. I had to take the cross off and sleep with it clutched in my fist." She took

THE ALTAR IN THE CHAPEL AT ST. BENEDICT'S ABBEY, SCENE OF BOTH OF LINDA'S DELIVERANCES.

the cross off and demonstrated for me, winding the black cord through her fingers, showing me how she slept with the cross in her fist, the cord twined securely around her fingers like a one-handed cat's cradle. It's the cross of Saint Benedict, and the protection Linda gets from it is powerful. The cross is silver, filled in with black enamel, a quietly elegant piece. Behind the crucified Christ is the medal of Saint Benedict, with a Latin prayer of exorcism etched into the perimeter of the medal.

"To this day, I keep a cross over my bed wherever I sleep. Father Jose gave me a bigger cross too, and that hangs permanently over my bed. Jerry even installed a small hook over my side of the bed in the motorhome, so that I can hang a cross there when we travel."

Even after Linda's deliverance, the demons didn't want to let go.

"I was at the abbey for a meal. Everyone was downstairs in the kitchen, sitting around the table, just chatting and having a great time. But I was in agony. The demons were screaming at me, screaming in my ears, all three of them. *"Give us your soul! You're lost! You're damned!"* I couldn't concentrate, I couldn't hear anything that was going on, nothing besides this shouting. I was in tears. Imagine trying to have a conversation with someone, and having three drill sergeants shouting at you at the same time."

She got up and blindly fumbled her way halfway up the stairs, leaning against the wall on the landing. *I can't take any more of this,* she thought. She struggled the rest of the way up the stairs, shoved the door open, and stumbled out to her car.

She yanked the car door open and fell into the seat, blinded by tears, her ears and mind still ringing with the demonic screams. *What happened? I thought I was safe! Father Jose and the bishop prayed for me ... but it didn't work! Please, Lord, why didn't it work?* She prayed, letting her heartache spill from her.

"Lord, you promised you wouldn't send me any more than I could stand. You *promised.* I can't stand this. Please, please help me!"

A gentle knock on the window roused her. Fr. Jose peered in at her, concern flooding his dark eyes. "Linda, what's wrong?"

"He could see I was just devastated. I said, 'Father, I can't stand this. They're just screaming at me, they won't leave me alone.' Then all the monks came and prayed over me. It was like the demons had to back off then. That's what finally did it. That's what I needed – a complete drenching in prayer."

Fr. Jose coaxed Linda out of the car, and together they walked back up to the church. He led her to the tiny Blessed Sacrament chapel again, and this time, all the monks of the abbey joined them in prayer. The demonic shrieking stopped then, dying down to a whisper.

After several months of prayer and help, Fr. Jose felt comfortable enough to share something very strange with Linda.

"We've grown closer now," he said during one conversation, "and I want to share something with you. The day we met, I was on my way to a luncheon appointment when Bishop Morales came and got me to talk to you. I didn't have an appointment with you – at one o'clock or at any other time."

Linda's brow furrowed in confusion. "But I called. A man told me to come see you, specifically, at one pm. I came early because I just couldn't wait."

"If you had waited, I would have been gone. Linda, I asked every monk in this place. *No one* had taken a phone call from you. You didn't talk to any monk here."

To add to the strangeness, every monk at the abbey is Hispanic, and has a Puerto Rican accent. The man Linda spoke to on the phone had no trace of an accent.

Linda's voice holds a chill of wonder. "I talked to an angel. I think I talked to an angel who led me to Fr. Jose and the bishop at just the right time, when the bishop was leaving, bouncing his keys in his hand on his way to the car. If I had waited until one pm, when my appointment was scheduled, they both would have been gone. I truly believe I talked to an angel, and so does Fr. Jose. Because no one else was there."

21. "THERE LURKS THE SKID DEMON"

So, how does one fix a demonic problem?

For those of a spiritual bent, there are many ways to counteract demonic influence. Linda didn't find any relief from exorcism, but the prayers of deliverance helped her. Pentecostals all over the United States firmly believe in the use of deliverance ministry. For those of a more superstitious mind, there are other options. Practitioners of Pennsylvania Dutch hex magic make a good living on the side by removing hexes.

In Asian cultures, though, the attitude is quite different. There's a good bit of hard-headed pragmatism at work in the East when it comes to demons.

The entrance to most Buddhist temples is guarded by statues of demons. To enter the sacred space, you have to walk directly between these fierce guardians. This is because all humans have to come to terms with their own demons – the demons of fear, ignorance, temptation, aggression, and a host of others. If we want to live a sacred life, we have to get a grip on these demons.

Buddhism has the story of an 11th century teacher, a woman named Machig Labdron (c. 1055 – c. 1145). Machig is the only woman credited with starting her own spiritual practice, which she called Chod (pronounced "chuh"), which means "to cut through". The practice involves visualizing one's demons – addiction, perfectionism, anger, self-hatred, anything that is dragging you down or draining your energy – then feeding those demons and turning them into allies.

The idea behind the practice comes from a story told about Machig Labdron herself. Machig was meditating with several of her spiritual sisters, when in a state of deep meditation, she rose from where she was sitting and levitated about a foot off the ground. Still in a deep trance, she passed through the walls of the temple and flew into a tree that stood next to a small pond outside the monastery.

The pond was the home of a naga, or water demon. These spirits are believed to have a dual nature – if they are disturbed, they can attack, causing disease and other problems. But if they are honored, they can act as protectors, even guardians of treasure. The naga of this particular pond was so terrifying that the local people wouldn't dare go near the water, superstitiously refusing even to look at it. But that's where Machig ended up, still meditating. She perched in the branches of the tree and stayed there in a state of serene bliss.

The naga of the pond considered Machig's arrival a confrontation. He rose up and threatened her, but she stayed in the tree's branches, still deep in happy meditation. This infuriated the demon, so he gathered the spirits from all over the area to attack Machig. When she saw the army of demons swarming towards her, Machig transformed her body into an offering of food.

The nagas were overwhelmed by this show of compassion. Not only did they back off, they committed themselves to Machig. They promised to protect her and to serve her and anyone who followed her teachings. By meeting the demons without fear and offering herself as food with steadfast compassion rather than trying to fight them, Machig turned the demons from enemies into allies.

This is a particularly Eastern attitude towards demons. The word "daemon" in Greek originally referred to a person's guiding spirit. The Greek daemon was a spiritual creature, something a person could trust, an entity to be relied on for divine guidance. In the West, Christian beliefs forced a change in this attitude as Christianity attacked pagan sensibilities. By the Middle Ages, demons were denounced as evil, and blamed for every misfortune, from illness to accidents to the miseries of the world.

This branch of Buddhism, though, teaches that by feeding your demons with compassion during meditation, you can turn them from demons back into daemons. The enemy can be transformed into an ally.

The zar ritual of the Middle East is another way of working with demons. The zar is not so much an exorcism as it is a negotiation, between the human and the djinn who possesses her. The djinn is an excuse to ask for sweets, pretty clothes, or exquisite perfumes. The family and friends of the possessed woman offer these gifts to the djinn, in its shell of human. It's a form of reconciliation, rather than confrontation and release.

The Western attitude is more proactive. We speak of "fighting our demons", whether figurative or literal. We fall prey to things like "demon rum". We say that our demons get a hold on us when we drink (for example), and bad things happen. In this mindset, Satan works as God's enforcer, God's punisher, the heavy who smacks a crowbar meditatively against the flat of his palm while eyeing your kneecaps. He's God's clean-up guy. For us Westerners, it's a way to explain personal responsibility.

And to help us face up to this accountability, we employ exorcists. Christians are encouraged to consider demons as undesirable trespassers. A trespasser is someone who unlawfully encroaches on someone else's property. They continue their unlawful squatting until someone with authority comes along and evicts them. They need to be challenged on the basis of one's legal rights. We feel the need to have someone in our corner as we struggle, someone with authority, someone who can act as a bouncer for the guys who are fouling up the party. Someone who can say, "Satan's messing it up for everyone here. Satan, you need to leave, and you know what? Take your friends with you. And don't come back." We need to have someone we can go to and say, "Look, my body and mind are under attack, and I need this loud, foulmouthed jerk bounced."

The only problem is that you have to get a bouncer who can do the job. Demons have had eternity to study us, to see what makes humans tick. It's like playing chess with a master – the master's not likely to give an inch, or let you go for best two out of three. Demonic lore is littered with stories of humans who have made a deal with the devil, and come up woefully short.

There is yet another way of looking at Lucifer in particular. Traditional Christian dogma sees Lucifer as a fallen angel, and not much more. In New Age thought, however, Lucifer has a much more nuanced role. He represents the energies of creative selfishness and self-awareness. We need self-awareness in order to evolve enough to unite with the Universe, or to put it another way, to join with the Divine.

Lucifer represents the energy of pride, of self-love, of selfishness, and of awareness of one's personal identity. These all can have positive results for our personal development. Humanity thrives on things like self-respect, self-worth, and self-identity. It is when we focus solely on ourselves, when we make self-love our most important emotion, which we run into trouble spiritually. In order to make full use of the evolutionary advantages offered by self-knowledge, we have to make sure that there is a flow to our self-love. We have to acknowledge that every other human experiences this self-love too.

This is why some see "hell" as being a state of isolation. If these energies are blocked, if self-awareness is simply turned inward, spiritual growth and evolution just doesn't happen. And Lucifer, as the bearer and the instigator of these energies, is right there with us. He follows us down into this "hell". He encourages this negative energy until we say, "Okay, that's it, I've had enough of this darkness." Lucifer pushes us to go beyond ourselves. Lucifer is the angel of experience. He's the angel of change, and we humans balk at change.

Lucifer (as opposed to Satan) is neither good nor bad. He is completely neutral. He is another agent of God, just like Christ. He is the agent that pushes us toward evolution, towards thinking for ourselves. He is the agent that helps us to realize the power of our own creative manifestation.

Lucifer also demands that we think for ourselves, and that we take responsibility for what we manifest for ourselves. We're human, we're fallible. We do the best we can, but sometimes we get mired in the ruts of our own minds. We make mistakes. And those mistakes manifest as stagnation, as bad luck, as "oh, the Universe hates me". We can do better. We can manifest joy for ourselves.

Christ stands ready to receive us into the Light. But it is Lucifer, the Light-bearer, who points us in that direction. It's not only that Lucifer and Christ are two sides of the same coin. It goes deeper than that. Without Lucifer's guidance and encouragement, we won't evolve enough to appreciate God.

22. LIFE GOES ON

Linda still hears the voices of the damned.

It's like if you have pneumonia – once your lungs are damaged by the infection, you are more susceptible ever after. The voices are faint, and most of the time Linda is pretty good at ignoring them. But they are still there, away in the background.

They are still there.

Linda still does battle with these spirits. At one time, she was afraid that the dark trinity could read her mind. She would be reading her devotions, and they would taunt her as she read. "*You don't believe that, do you? Not really.*" Her faith shook, but stayed solid.

Through many painful months, Linda came to an astonishing realization – one that changed her life. The realization was quite simple: evil spirits cannot read your mind. However, they can convince you that they can, by manipulating your thoughts and playing on your deepest fears.

Linda's advice is simple. When you are troubled, do as Hannah did – pray silently. Hannah was the mother of the Old Testament prophet Samuel. She was chastised for praying aloud in the Temple, so she took to praying silently, so as not to incur the displeasure of the Temple priests. As Linda says, "Pray silently to God, and arise victorious, not a victim.' That's how I've come to where I am today. When I hear something that's not true, I picture Christ's hands, and I just set it in there, and I know that they have no control over me, and I am at peace. Sometimes I still hear these entities, but it's like they're a thousand miles away. Sometimes I still see them, but instead of acknowledging them, I'll picture Christ's hands."

As strange as it may seem, Linda is actually grateful for the hell she has been through in the past two years. Because of this whole experience, she says, her husband has been baptized, and she and her husband were both confirmed in the Church. Jerry had no idea what was going on – only that his wife needed help.

"He could see me going through something that he didn't understand. He could hear me screaming at these things that he couldn't see. He knew that I was changing and he didn't understand it at all. But he knew that I needed help."

Because of this, her son in Texas became a believer, and her son in Morton, Illinois, sought out his minister.

"He went to the church and said, 'I think my mom's going loco – she's hearing these voices.' The minister explained the situation to him so that his spiritual growth was deepened. What the spirits intended for evil, God intended for good. God turned all that evilness around."

Linda no longer hunts ghosts. She has had her fill of the paranormal world. Yet she still aches to help those afflicted by evil spirits. As she puts it, "I want to live in the supernatural, but not the paranormal. I want to work with the supernatural gifts of the Holy Spirit. But I don't want to experience any more of the paranormal. I don't wish that on anyone."

There is a difference, Linda says, between the supernatural and the paranormal. As she explains it, the supernatural comes from God. Supernatural events could include faith healing, an angelic warning of impending danger, or the feel of Michael's wings enveloping Linda in times of stress. The paranormal, on the other hand, is simply an event caused by something humans can't see. The paranormal doesn't necessarily have anything to do with God. It's just something unexplainable.

"I will never look at anyone who says they hear voices the same way again. Yes, I'm going to make sure they're not crazy, not [schizophrenic]. I'll clear all that out of the way first ... but I know it's real. I know that there's a battle that needs to be fought."

The Slender Man stabbing case, for example, is something that really resonates with Linda, given all that she has been through in the past years. Payton Leutner, a twelve year old girl, was attacked in a wooded park near Waukesha, Wisconsin in May 2014. She was stabbed nineteen times – by her classmates.

These girls, also pre-teens, spent months planning the attack on Payton. They did it, they told police, to curry favor with a fictional character, a monster called Slender Man. This boogeyman was made up by writers on the website Something Awful. The phantom originated in a Photoshop contest in the Something Awful forums in 2009. From there, it was picked up by a website that was a gathering place for harmless, but scary, Internet urban legends. According to the *Daily Mail*, Slender Man is often depicted as an unnaturally tall, thin figure with a blank, featureless face, who wears a black suit. His arms are long, outstretched to capture and terrorize his prey, usually children. The phantasm is said to be able to teleport and to create distortions in photographs.

All of this could be shrugged off as one of thousands of Internet memes, were it not for the very real repercussions of the Slender Man's existence. Payton's two classmates became obsessed with Slender Man. One of the girls even claimed that the phantom would visit her in dreams, and that he lived in a mansion in the Nicolet National Forest. The girls crafted a plan to attract the notice of the phantom. They lured Payton to a park in Waukesha, where they stabbed her nineteen times, piercing her liver, pancreas, and stomach, and barely missing an artery near her heart. Payton miraculously was able to crawl to a nearby sidewalk, where a passing cyclist saw her and called the police.

The influence of Slender Man is not limited to one isolated occurrence in Wisconsin. In Hamilton County, Ohio, a woman was stabbed by her thirteen year old daughter. She suffered several cuts on her face and neck, with a particularly deep gash on her back. The woman said that her daughter appeared to be in a trance during the attack, as though she had been brainwashed.

And a fourteen year old girl in Port Richey, Florida, set fire to her house, knowing that her mother and brother were asleep inside. After an argument with her mother over household chores, the teen disappeared for several hours. The mother and brother woke later to the screech of a smoke alarm and billowing flames. They escaped the blaze unhurt, but badly shaken. The mother later got an unnerving text from the teen. "Mom, I'm so sorry. I don't know why I did it. Did any of [you] get hurt?"

The folk historian and writer Michael Kleen has an intriguing theory about the horrifying Slender Man cases. His question is simple and chilling: are the creators of this character legally liable for murder?

"Whenever tragic events of this nature happen, we naturally look for something to blame. It is rare (though not unheard of) for girls at this young age to commit murder or attempted murder. So we ask why? What drove these girls to brutally attack their friend? Was it bad parenting? Violent video games? Heavy metal music? The girls themselves said they did it 'to become proxies for Slender Man.' Apparently, they believed that if they were to stab their friend to death, Slender Man would appear and prove he was real to skeptics. Since Slender Man is a fictional supernatural being created by Something Awful forum members in 2009, some people might place the blame on its creators. They would argue that this attack never would have happened without the Slender Man mythology. Its creators might even be held legally responsible if it's shown that their art explicitly encouraged people to take violent action.

"The problem, however, is that the Slender Man mythos has been perpetuated and elaborated on by hundreds of people. Although in retrospect there appears to be a clear connection between Slender Man's creation in 2009 and this horrific crime, there is no way its creators could have predicted these actions. There is never any way of telling how mentally and emotionally disturbed individuals will react to anything in popular culture. I'm confident that if these girls hadn't used Slender Man as an excuse to attack their friend, they would have found a different reason. Humans have used supernatural entities to justify horrific behavior for thousands of years. Slender Man, although he was created in our digital world, is no different."

Linda has her own theories on the Slender Man stabbing. "I really think those young girls were hearing demonic voices, voices that convinced them to do something violent." There have been many such cases of demonic influence. This situation just happens to have a source that we can trace.

Linda no longer considers herself a paranormal investigator. Her group, Central Illinois Ghost Hunters, has gone through many internal changes, and the structure is radically different from the group that she co-founded.

"Part of it makes me sad because I worked *so* hard to build up that group. We were so well-known, and so professional. I even had someone from Canada call me about a missing-persons case."

But all that – the interviews with frightened homeowners, the setting up of equipment, the hours upon hours of reviewing evidence – that's all in Linda's past now. Her focus has changed.

"It's not my business any more. My business now is to help people. Will I go on investigations and [ask the spirits] 'Are you John Jones?' No, I don't do that any more. But will I go in and pray for the lost spirits in a house? Absolutely. I pray, whatever's in this house, be released and go to the Father, or if it's something bad, go to the foot of the Cross and remain there until Christ decides what to do with you. That's what I need to be doing. I am to help people. I am to listen to them, I'm to give them help and comfort, to tell them they're not alone. But I'm not going to put a flashlight down and ask questions. Not any more."

Even with all she has been through, Linda still feels the pull to help people. She and her husband were sitting at a restaurant having lunch when she realized that their waitress was off her game somehow. Linda didn't feel it was her place to pry, so she tried to resist the urge to ask the waitress what was wrong. But the woman seemed so despondent ... Linda accepts her gifts of discernment and empathy, so she finally decided to act.

"What's wrong?" she asked.

After a few minutes of gentle encouragement, the waitress shared her story. Her son had found a Book of Shadows that had belonged to his grandmother. He and his girlfriend had taken the book to a local cemetery and had used it to call up something very nasty. The boy said that ever since then, he could see a dark, menacing shape waiting for him in a corner, patiently stalking him.

"Can you help him?" the waitress pleaded.

Linda felt drawn to help the woman. She could tell the waitress was drowning in sadness and worry for her son. But she was still wary of any contact, however slight, with the forces of evil. Regretfully, she told the woman she couldn't get involved.

Linda's ordeal has made her even more sensitive to the beings that exist in the shadowy spaces between worlds. She has noticed that more figures, like the dark phantom that scared the mailman in Mackinaw, are appearing in houses – not necessarily doing anything, just showing up. Her theory is that there is a "thinning of the realms" taking place. Perhaps with all the modern interest in the paranormal, the boundaries between this world and the next are getting hazy.

During CIGH's investigation of the Satanist's house in Springfield, Linda caught an intriguing EVP. It was a woman's voice, firm but gentle, saying, "*Let me pass; I am a Watcher*".

Linda was fascinated by this calm voice. Ever since then, she has been curious about this spirit. Was it an active participant, watching the battle between good and evil, waiting for the chance to jump in and shift the balance of power? And in which direction? Or was it simply watching dispassionately? The words "*let me pass*" are a mystery – was the spirit simply watching over the investigative team, protecting them from any malignance in the house? Or was the spirit on its way to harm the team? We may never know.

Through her experiences, Linda has found the reassurance that so many paranormal investigators seek, the reason many of them take up the practice. She is now absolutely, thoroughly, unshakably convinced that there is an afterlife.

When Linda's mother was dying, she would tell Linda that she'd seen family members waiting to welcome her to the Other Side. These visitations were just as much a joyous comfort to Linda as they were to her mother.

"I saw Uncle Houston today! He was so glad to see me – he says that when I get there, he's going to make me a big dinner!" Every day, she would say, "I found this one," or "I saw So-and-so today." The meetings, and the promised reunions, seemed to give her much-needed strength for the final journey.

Two nights before she died, Linda's mother had a sobering report. "Uncle Houston came and told me he can't help me any more, that I have to do this on my own, but that he'll be there waiting for me." Two nights later, Linda's mother took that final step all on her own. Linda knows, deep down in her soul where it really counts, that Uncle Houston and the whole family were there to meet her and welcome her to her next great adventure.

"We know there's an afterlife," Linda says with quiet conviction. "It's not just chemicals in the brain. We know there's good, we know there's evil."

As far as the spirits themselves are concerned, Linda remains ambivalent. Are there any good spirits out there? Or are they evil spirits just pretending to be good? She's been burned before, and she is predictably reluctant to commit to an answer, even in her own mind. She's still working it through.

"That's where I am in my walk right now. I'm trying to decipher it – are these things really good? Or are they things pretending to be good to draw us in? And most importantly, can we really help people who are suffering the same way I did? Because if it happened to me, it has happened to other people. I'm not special. I'm just one child – there are millions. It has strengthened my faith. It has brought me to the realization that there are others who need help. We need to be helping them, because most people won't believe them.

"I was talking with Father Harold [at the monastery] one day, and he said something really profound. 'There are different dimensions,' he said. 'We don't go into theirs ... but they certainly do come into ours.'"

Linda has a particularly difficult time explaining to herself the apparition of the little boy who appeared during her first visit to the monastery. Bishop Morales felt that the child was attached to Linda because of the maternal instinct he sensed in her. He encouraged Linda to communicate with the boy. "Tell him to go to the Father, that He can care for him better than you ever could." Then, Linda, Fr. Jose, and the bishop all heard a child's voice say, *Thank you.*

The presence of this young child's spirit may hold a clue to Linda's demonic attachment. In his blog, *Phantoms and Monsters*, the paranormal expert Lon Strickler describes the chilling case of a poltergeist known as the Sioux City Entity. "This is the point where the overwhelming spirit energy at the location comes into play. As a result of the crash of United Airlines Flight 232, there are many wandering spirits in the vicinity ... many of which don't realize that they are no longer part of a living body or remain for other reasons.

"Malevolent entities require energy to remain viable. If they cannot feed on human emotion and life force, then they need to look elsewhere. Earthbound spirits are fodder for stronger entities...and this was the reason it became so difficult to weaken this troublesome entity."

So we are faced with yet another intriguing question. Since Linda spent several intense years ghost hunting, and many years before that simply being receptive to the supernatural, is it possible that several traumatized spirits, like the ghost of the young boy, attached themselves to her without her knowledge? Was their presence simply masked by the overwhelming energy of the three demons? Is this why it was so incredibly difficult for Linda to find lasting relief from their torment?

"I have a little box in my mind, where I put everything that doesn't make sense. Someday, if the time is ever right, the Lord will explain it to me. I can't imagine that that little boy represents something bad, but ... I don't know that it was something good."

Linda is terribly gun-shy when it comes to spirits now. When I ventured, "This indecision must be very frustrating for you," she immediately answered "Yes, because of my gifts." I can't imagine how frustrating it must be, to have the gift of being able to sense spirits, but to be hesitant to reach out to help them, in case the spirit isn't as innocuous as a little boy wanting his mama.

Fr. Jose understands Linda's ambivalence towards the world of the paranormal. He knows of her reasons for telling her story, for getting the word out about her terrifying experiences. He knows she wants to warn people about the dangers of stumbling into this sort of situation.

"I agree with her, because people start messing with these things and they don't know what they're getting into. Take Linda herself as an example – she was very well-intentioned, but it really backfired on her. That's why the Church is so very cautious when it comes to investigating claims of demonic possession. The Church does a lot of careful investigation before agreeing to perform an exorcism. We look at the person's background, there are psychological evaluations ... there's a lot that goes into it. You have to have permission from the bishop to do that. Normally, there's a priest that is assigned to be the exorcist of the diocese. That priest's identity is kept under wraps, for his own protection."

This isn't done only to keep attention-seeking weirdos away from the parish. There is actually a very good reason to keep an exorcist's identity on the down-low – and it isn't only to keep the human predators at bay.

"If you expose the name of the priest that performs the exorcisms, you're actually putting him in harm's way, because then the demons can concentrate a full attack on that particular priest. An exorcist has to be very grounded in prayer. It's taken very seriously."

So how do we know if what we are facing is a demonic entity, or not? Linda suggests a good rule of thumb, shared with her by an old preacher many years ago. "If you are experiencing fear, total complete fear, that's something evil. That's of the Devil, because he does not know how to give you peace and love. He can't even imitate those things." Being startled, he said, is not the same thing. After all, Mary was startled by the angel Gabriel, but she wasn't fearful. When you see something and you're not afraid, that could be something that's not necessarily demonic.

I asked Linda about the brush of angelic feathers against her arms. "So was that really the Archangel Michael? Or do you still think that was the demon masquerading as Michael? You said you weren't scared, that you felt peace and reassurance."

She was silent for a few long moments. Then she spoke, hesitation in her voice. "Again, it's all about discernment. You have to trust in the gift of discernment, of being able to tell the difference. That could really have been Michael or another angel protecting me, instead of a demon faking it."

The question uppermost in her mind is simple and plaintive in its clarity. Why did God allow her to suffer so horrendously for over two years? She has mulled this question over and over, discussing it with ministers, bringing it to her God in prayer. Finally, she decided that God did it for one simple reason: to let the world know that these dark entities are real.

The case that still haunts her is the teenage girl in Springfield, the one who worships Diana. Central Illinois Ghost Hunters had been called to the house because the young daughter of the family was having trouble sleeping. The nightmares were so intense that she would wake up screaming. When asked, the ten-year-old innocently admitted to worshipping Diana, the huntress and moon goddess of Greek mythology. Students learn Diana's story in fifth grade, along with the tales of the other gods and goddesses of the Greek pantheon. As a representation of strong, independent womanhood, Diana would hold a certain appeal to a smart young girl.

"That was four years ago. That little girl would be a teenager now. She said she heard voices … and I just wonder if she's going through the same torment I did. I just wonder if she's okay."

Linda can see the hand of God reaching back through the years of her life. Her experience at the Golden Acres Church of the Nazarene was just the beginning of her life-long journey. It was that experience, back when she was nine years old, which laid the foundation for the spirituality that would carry her for the rest of her life. It was that experience that made her realize, decades later, that her trials with the demons couldn't be undone with a simple handshake. She needed the laying on of hands, the sensation of being covered in prayer. Her childhood revelation taught her something else, too, many years down her path.

"When you pray, when you accept that grace, you're filled with the Holy Spirit, and I believe that there is no condemnation of those that love the Lord. You can ask for forgiveness, and you will be forgiven."

She feels that by opening herself up in prayer, she let God into her life. And God has guided her ever since. That near-drowning in the Illinois River when Linda was fourteen? She thinks – knows – that those moments she spent underwater could have gone very differently.

"I look back, and I think, my goodness, when I was fourteen, down by the river … that might not have turned out the same way if I hadn't prayed when I was nine. And even if that hadn't happened, there was the guy that came into Ripper and Associates, the man I had to call 911 about. I think those are the kinds of things God saved me from, because I was obedient when I was a kid."

Sure, Linda was religious before this experience. She went to church. She read the Bible. She believed in God. But her fight with the feral trinity took that faith and forced it to put down roots, deep taproots that anchored her soul in the promise of God's all-encompassing love for the faithful.

"Here's the reason this all happened. God said to me, I'm going to take you on this journey. You're going to feel like you're not going to make it … but I am always there with you. Every time I look back on what I went through, God was right there, all the time. He would only let the spirits go so far, then He'd step in."

Even now, she can still hear the whispers of the demons in the night. When she does, when she wakes in the darkness and hears the menacing growls and mutters of her tormentors, she will remind herself of the truth. "Linda? What is truth? The truth is, there is God the Father who chose you before Time began. What is truth? God sent his only-begotten Son to die, that you should have Eternal Life. What is truth? You are covered in the Blood of Christ, that washes away all the sins that you did, have done, or ever will do, as long as you are repentant. What is truth? The Holy Spirit comes to live in me, and I am sealed by the Holy Spirit until the Day of Redemption. When I start listening to their lies, I tell myself, what is truth?, and I tell myself what I'm thankful for."

We know that the only way a demon can take over a person is by invitation. Here is where Linda had an undeniable advantage. She never ever gave the dark spirits permission to take over her soul, not once. She fought with the assurance of having God on her side, even when she couldn't sense His presence in the depths of her despair. She resisted giving in to the demons' torment with every ounce of her strength. "When I look back on all of this, I realize that God had different people helping to lead me to the Abbey."

Donna, with her misidentification of the praying monk; Mike, who was willing to pray long-distance with Linda at any hour of the day – or night; the various priests who tried in their own misguided way to help her ... everyone was part of the larger picture. Even Al, as annoying as he was, had a part to play.

"As I was trying to tell Fr. Jose what was going on, that day we had our first phone conversation, Al kept interrupting, telling his own version of things. I was in such deep need, I could hardly think, and he was just not helping. It's kind of ironic, if you really think about it. God used Al to put me in contact with Fr. Jose, then Al got all annoying. Looking back, though, I can see that it was all part of the process. If I could have talked without interruption, I would have gone to see Fr. Jose right away. I wouldn't have gone through that whole process of learning. So even Al's obnoxious interruptions were part of God's plan."

Even the loss of Central Illinois Ghost Hunters, and all of her friends, had its lessons for her. "God removed them from my life," Linda admits. "If he hadn't, I would have continued to go on investigations with them, and I would have continued to be in that environment. I had to cut the ties. I had to remove myself completely from them, and from that environment."

This sudden break from her friends, from the familiarity of investigation, from the predictability of her life – all that, Linda feels, was vitally necessary to her journey closer to God. Painful, at times agonizing, but necessary. "I couldn't have done it any other way. I had to be ready to receive their help, at the time it came along."

The way Linda made her way to the Abbey is a miracle in itself. "Through seven priests, through two exorcisms, through a mistake by a friend, through another friend getting a priest on the phone, and me saying, 'Father, don't forget me', and him praying for me every day ... it's amazing how the Lord led me through all that. It took a month and a half of searching to find Fr. Jose to help me."

It's curious, too, that the monks at the Abbey were the only ones that were able to help her. Others listened to her tribulations, but they kept her at arm's length. Fr. Jose and Bishop Morales, though, waded into the fight right next to Linda and shielded her, laying hands on her and drenching her in prayer. Linda has a theory that because all of the monks at the Abbey are of Hispanic descent, they are more receptive to the idea of spiritual battle. Their culture makes allowances for the supernatural, for experiences outside the norm. We can look at the joyful, exuberant Latino celebration of Dia de los Muertos as an example.

El Dia de los Muertos (Day of the Dead) is a celebration of life, respectful of the dead and laced with humor. The dead are honored on November 1 and 2 – All Saints' Day and All Souls' Day in the church calendar. The Day of the Dead evolved from the 12th century Aztec festival dedicated to Mictecacihuatl, the Lady of the Underworld who guarded the bones of the deceased. With the coming of the Spanish explorers in the 15th century, pre-Columbian traditions merged with Catholic rituals to form a rich tapestry of folk culture. People make calavera (sugar skulls) and pan de muerto (sweet egg bread shaped in the form of arm or leg bones). These sweets are used to decorate graves and home altars, or given as gifts. The festival is a happy celebration of life and what comes afterwards – after all, death comes to everyone, and hopefully we can learn not to fear it. For a few days at the tail end of fall, the boundaries between everyday life and the supernatural are blurred.

Also, the monks, Father Abbot, and the bishop may be inclined to be spiritual warriors simply by virtue of having chosen the Benedictine order. The medal of Saint Benedict has a special meaning for those intrigued by exorcism. The most popular of these medals in honor of the saint is the Jubilee Medal of Montecassino. This medal was designed in 1880 with the supervision of the monks of Montecassino to celebrate the 1400th anniversary of the saint's birth.

The medal incorporates symbolism from the life of Saint Benedict, and of Christianity in general. On the face of the medal is the image of the saint holding a cross in his right hand, and a copy of his Rule for Monasteries in his left hand. To the saint's right is a broken cup. Worldly monks, dissatisfied with Saint Benedict's rigorous rules, decided to poison the saint. When he made the sign of the cross over the poisoned cup, the goblet shattered. To the left of the saint is a raven, about to carry away a loaf of poisoned bread that an enemy had sent.

The back of the medal is equally intriguing. A cross dominates the scene. In it are the initial letters of a Latin prayer that fairly dances with rhythm: *Crux sacra sit mihi lux! Numquam draco sit mihi dux!* ("May the holy cross be my light – may the dragon never be my guide.") The angels formed by the cross hold the letters CSPB, for *Crux sancti patris Benedicti* (the Cross of our holy father Benedict). Above the cross is the word *pax* (peace), a Benedictine motto.

In 1647, a manuscript dating to 1415 was found at the Abbey of Metten in Bavaria which explained the letters on the medal as the initials of a Latin prayer of exorcism. Around the edge of the medal's reverse are the initial letters of this ancient prayer. VRSNSMV – SMQLIVB. *Vade retro Satana! Numquam suade mihi vana! Sunt mala quae libas. Ipse venena bibas!* The translation of this lilting Latin is equally powerful: "Begone Satan! Never tempt me with your vanities! What you offer me is evil. Drink the poison yourself!"

This brazen incantation is an intrinsic part of the Benedictine medal. It is, in fact, the only religious medal with an exorcism prayer etched right on it. Perhaps the monks at the abbey had internalized this reminder of Satan's vanquishing, and that is why they were able to so confidently lay hands on Linda and send her demons packing.

Linda bears no ill-will towards any of the people who couldn't help her. She can even understand the rejection of the charismatic group, as much as it stung at the time.

"I was judging them for not helping me, and I shouldn't have done that. They were just scared. That lady who touched my forehead – she was scared to death at the thought of attracting the attention of the demons I had around me. I could feel the power of the Lord in her touch. I told Dick she could be a powerful prayer warrior … but she's scared. She doesn't want that torment. And I don't know how her demons tormented her – maybe she could see them in her room at night or something. Maybe that's why she said 'you lizard-looking thing'. It was bad enough for me hearing them … I sure wouldn't want to see them."

Linda no longer thinks that her experiences were a punishment. Instead, she realizes that they were a way for God to impart knowledge to her – to say, "Hey, Linda, this stuff is *real*. You need to tell people that this is real."

In spite of all the agony she went through – or perhaps because of it – Linda has never given up on her desire to help those afflicted by evil entities. It's something intrinsic to her, a part of her nature. She's still working on that, she says, with Fr. Jose and Bishop Morales.

"These evil spirits – these things hate us. I mean *hate. Us.* It's hard to fathom how supremely evil these things are. They hate us with a passion that can't even be imagined. My mission is to help those that are going through this, to let them know that they are not alone, that there is hope, that they're going to make it through. They have to hold on, they have to persevere … but they *can* make it through. God *will* help them make it through. There's nothing that they've ever done that He cannot undo.

"He promises us, Though your sins be as crimson, I will wash you and make you as white as snow. All these things that the evil spirits accuse us of, even down to the tiniest little white lies that we've forgotten about … it's washed. If you ask for forgiveness, it's as though these sins never existed. We're clean. We stand holy before God.

"The Bible says, 'We fight not against flesh and blood, but against spiritual wickedness in high places.' And I can attest to that. It is true, it is true, it is true. I've been through it."

CONCLUSION

One night, as I was deeply into writing this book, I dreamed about it. I was working on it so much that naturally, it slipped into my subconscious. (I've suffered a couple of really nasty nightmares while working on it too, but that's not what I want to tell you about.)

In part of the dream, I was having a conversation with Father Jose, the abbot priest who helped Linda with her deliverance. In the dream, he was sitting behind a desk, while I was in a chair opposite. A copy of this book lay on the desk between us; other than that, the hardwood surface of the desk was bare. Fr. Jose picked up the book, then tossed it back down on the desk with a look of confused irritation.

"You've given me this book on spiritual warfare, but it doesn't tell me how to fight demons – it's just a story," he complained.

Almost immediately after that, as I was lying in bed drowsing through the waking-up process and revisiting the night's dreams in my mind, I had another dream – or more accurately, a memory. I was still mostly asleep, so the lines between memory and dream were still deliciously blurred.

I have always had wretched eyesight. I started wearing glasses in second grade. In fourth grade, the eye doctor had me do some exercises in an attempt to strengthen my eyesight. The contraption I took home was a gray plastic stand with cards on it. The cards were about a foot and a half away from my eyes when placed in their holder, and there were two images on each card, like a stereoscope. The idea was that I should focus on bringing those two images together to form one overlapping picture, and that would strengthen my eye muscles and improve my sight.

I don't think it was an accident that I had a dream-memory about that gadget right after the dream–Fr. Jose confronted me about the purpose of this book. I don't consider myself an expert on demons or Christianity or spiritual warfare. I don't claim expertise or superiority in any of these matters. I have simply told the story of Linda's demonic oppression as she told it to me. Along the way, I have tried to examine that part of our universe and our psyche that experiences demons.

This book is not a handbook for spiritual warfare. I don't presume to tell anyone how to conduct their religious life, if they have one. If you suspect that you are having demonic difficulties, please, please contact a priest or a religious person you feel comfortable talking to. Or get in touch with Linda at huntingdemons@yahoo.com.

Having said that, I'd like to think that I've been able to bring these two images together – the spiritual and the storytelling. And just as in fourth grade, it wasn't always easy to get those two images to merge together, but I hope I have managed to pull it off.

If you read this book hoping for spiritual enlightenment, I pray that it has pointed you in a direction that will be useful to you. And if you picked it up looking for a few hours' worth of entertainment, I trust I've delivered that.

A FINAL WORD: FROM LINDA K.

"For we fight not against flesh and blood, but against principalities, and powers, against the rulers of darkness of this world, against spiritual wickedness in high places." **Ephesians 6:12**

I thought I would be an investigator all my life. I knew without a doubt that this was my calling; I could use my gifts to help people and spirits to find freedom, peace and rest. Until the spirits I started encountering were no longer friendly, but evil and dark. In one split second, my life changed forever. I went from investigating the unknown to the unknown tormenting me.

My purpose for telling my story is in the hopes that I may help even one of you to consider and stop chasing Spirits before they catch you. There is a kingdom of the unknown that I would never have believed existed, even though the Bible scriptures warned of them; who truly believes that? I do now. **They exist.** They know everything you and I have ever done from the time we were born. These three spirits tormented me 24 hours 7 days a week for over two years. To this day they try at times to enter back into my consciousness; but for the Grace of God and the monks covering me in prayer, laying hands on me in intense prayer, I would not have made it through.

My hope is that after all I encountered and have gone through, that I may help those that are going through the same thing. Please be forewarned…do not ever try to pray out a house unless you have experience and training hopefully from the church….if you do….you may not like what you find or I should say what may find you.

ACKNOWLEDGEMENTS

I am so grateful to so many people who gave freely of their expertise to help me share Linda's story. Their contributions are the facets of the jewel, and this book shines because of them.

First there is Linda herself. I am so honored that she trusted me with this incredible story. Her quiet faith is an inspiration. She doesn't shout her Christianity from the rooftops, but instead serenely lives her faith every day. She takes each day as it comes. She will always be aware of her demons. But with her steadfast, utterly unshakeable conviction, I have no doubt that she will live a life rich with worship and praise.

Thanks also to Father Jose Reyes, Father Abbot at Saint Benedict's Abbey in Peoria. He welcomed me into his church, and freely shared this amazing story from his point of view.

I am also intensely grateful to the following people who lent me their stories and their vast talents: David Lowery, aka The Paranormal Highwayman, for his insight into his champion, Saint Michael the Archangel; Shelly Wilson and Nyree-Aine TheSeer, for the same; Michael Kleen, for allowing me to share his theory concerning legal questions surrounding the Slender Man crimes; and Lon Strickler, for being very generous with his time and his blog.

Thanks also to Troy Taylor, who coaxed this book to publication. I am pleased to call him my publisher, and I'm even prouder to call him my friend.

Troy is among the many folks in the paranormal world that I've had the pleasure to meet over the years. Mary Marshall, Lisa Taylor Horton, Rosemary Guiley, Ursula Bielski, Alexandra Holzer, Loren Hamilton, Len Adams, Luke Naliborski, Melissa Tanner, David Youngquist, Jeff Belanger, Dale Kaczmarek ... the list goes on. I used to think of these folks as my heroes. They still are ... but now they are my peers too, and I am profoundly glad for that.

A huge sloppy thank you goes out to all of the readers who asked for another book. You guys are the reason I plop my tushie in a chair and pound out the words. Without you, these books would not exist, and I owe you a million thanks and a ton of chocolate for letting me do this, and for being interested in the final product.

And the most important thank you of all goes to my husband Rob. I love you more than nachos.

BIBLIOGRAPHY

Addams, Jane. *Twenty Years at Hull House.* New York: The MacMillan Company, 1910.

_____. *The Second Twenty Years at Hull House.* New York: The MacMillan Company, 1930.

Allione, Tsultrim. *Feeding Your Demons: Ancient Wisdom for Resolving Inner Conflict.* New York: Little, Brown & Company, 2008.

Amorth, Fr. Gabriele. *An Exorcist Tells His Story.* Ignatius Press, 1999.

Baglio, Matt. *The Rite: The Making of a Modern Exorcist.* New York: Doubleday, 2009.

Bebergal, Peter. *Season of the Witch: How the Occult Saved Rock and Roll.* New York: Penguin Group, 2014.

Bielski, Ursula. *Chicago Haunts: Ghostlore of the Windy City.* Chicago: Lake Claremont Press, 1998.

Bobrow, Robert S. *The Witch in the Waiting Room: A Physician Investigates Paranormal Phenomena in Medicine.* New York: Thunder's Mouth Press, 2006.

Cuneo, Michael W. *American Exorcism: Expelling Demons in the Land of Plenty.* New York: Doubleday, 2001.

Drieskins, Barbara. *Living With Djinns: Understanding and Dealing With the Invisible in Cairo.* London: Saqi Books, 2008.

Echols, Damien. *Almost Home: My Life Story, Volume 1.* New York: iUniverse, 2004.

Goss, Linda and Marian E. Barnes (ed.). *Talk That Talk: An Anthology of African American Storytelling.* New York: Simon & Schuster, 1989.

Guiley, Rosemary Ellen. *The Djinn Connection.* New Milford, CT: Visionary Living, 2013.

_____. *The Encyclopedia of Demons and Demonology.* New York: Checkmark Books, 2009.

Hammond, Frank & Ida Mae. *Pigs in the Parlor: A Practical Guide to Deliverance.* Kirkwood, MO: Impact Books, 1973.

Harakas, Stanley Samuel. *Orthodox Christian Beliefs: Real Answers to Real Questions from Real People.* Minneapolis, MN: Light & Life Publishing Company, 2002.

Johnston, Jerry. *The Edge of Evil: The Rise of Satanism in North America.* Dallas, TX: Word Publishing, 1989.

LaVey, Anton Szandor. *The Satanic Bible.* New York: Avon Books, 1969.

Luhrmann, T.M. *When God Talks Back: Understanding the American Evangelical Relationship With God.* New York: Alfred A. Knopf, 2012.

Marcovitz, Hal. *Teens and the Supernatural and Paranormal.* Gallup Youth Survey: Major Issues and Trends. Broomall, PA: Mason Crest, 2014.
Martin, Malachi. *Hostage to the Devil: The Possession and Exorcism of Five Contemporary Americans.* New York: HarperOne, 1992.
McGrath, Malcolm. *Demons of the Modern World.* Amherst, NY: Prometheus Books, 2002.
Oesterreich, T.K. *Possession, Demoniacal and Other, Among Primitive Races in Antiquity, the Middle Ages, and Modern Times.* New York: University Books, 1966.
Ottens, Allen, and Rick Myer. *Coping With: Satanism: Rumor, Reality, and Controversy.* New York: The Rosen Publishing Group, 1998.
Patterson, R. Gary. *Take a Walk on the Dark Side: Rock and Roll Myths, Legends, and Curses.* New York: Fireside, 2004.
Peck, M. Scott, MD. *Glimpses of the Devil: A Psychiatrist's Personal Accounts of Possession, Exorcism, and Redemption.* New York: Free Press, 2005.
Pizzato, Mark. *Inner Theatres of Good and Evil: The Mind's Staging of Gods, Angels, and Devils.* Jefferson, NC: McFarland & Company, Inc, 2011.
Roleff, Tamara L., editor. *At Issue: Satanism.* San Diego, CA: Greenhaven Press, 2002.
Sakheim, David A. and Susan E. Devine. *Out of Darkness: Exploring Satanism and Ritual Abuse.* New York: Lexington Books (an imprint of Macmillan, Inc.), 1992.
Sarchie, Ralph and Lisa Collier Cool. *Deliver Us From Evil: A New York City Cop Investigates the Supernatural.* St. Martin's Griffin, 2014.
Schanzer, Rosalyn. *Witches! The Absolutely True Tale of Disaster in Salem.* Washington DC: National Geographic Society, 2013.
Schwartz, Ted and Duane Empey. *Satanism: Is Your Family Safe?* Grand Rapids, MI: Zondervan Publishing House, 1988.
Spangler, David. *Reflections on the Christ.* Moray, Scotland: Findhorn Publications, 1978.
Sugden, John. *Niccolo Paganini: Supreme Violinist or Devil's Fiddler?* Kent, Great Britain: Midas Books, 1980.
Taylor, Troy. *The Devil & All His Works: A History of Satan, Sin, Murder, Mayhem & Magic.* Decatur, IL: Whitechapel Press, 2013.
_____. *The Devil Came to St. Louis.* Decatur, IL: Whitechapel Press, 2006.
Victor, Jeffrey. *Satanic Panic: The Creation of a Contemporary Legend.* Peru, IL: Open Court Publishing Company, 1993.

Lights Out: Hunting Demons

In the darkness, how do you know who's hunting whom?

Linda was a seasoned paranormal investigator. Also a committed Christian, she prayed to be able to hear the lost souls with whom she was trying to communicate.

In this special episode of Lights Out, you'll hear Linda's terrifying true story of demonic oppression. Based on the book *Hunting Demons,* by Sylvia Shults, available from Whitechapel Press.

PRAY FOR THE GHOST HUNTERS —
PREY FOR THE GHOSTS.

Scan the QR code to hear this special episode of Lights Out. For more information, please visit prairieghosts.com, sylviashults.com, or Ghosts of the Illinois River on Facebook.

www.ingramcontent.com/pod-product-compliance
Lightning Source LLC
LaVergne TN
LVHW021119080426
835510LV00012B/1758